Advance Praise for

conversations of curriculum reform

"Educational autobiography can be done poorly or well—Kathryn M. Benson does it very well in this book. Using autobiography, hermeneutics, and phenomenology, Benson takes us through a rich, well-informed, and enlightening exploration of her consciousness as a teacher in Louisiana. This is curriculum theorizing at its best and should serve as a model for subsequent work in explorations of the lifeworld of teaching."

Joe L. Kincheloe, Canada Research Chair,
Faculty of Education, McGill University

"Kathryn M. Benson's work boldly inquires into the heart of educational life via the voices of those most impacted by it—students and their experiences of curriculum and schooling. Intrigued by the 'embodied possibilities that draw' her to the classroom and the 'existential relation experienced in the pedagogical' act, Benson locates the source of school reform, and educational transformation in the voice and agency of students and teachers as well as in their mutual quest for understanding. This provocative book eloquently illuminates the lives of 'teachers and students held by threads of desire and distancing' as together they 'wander the borders of meaning' in uncovering and recovering their educational lives through reading and rewriting the texts of their own lives."

Molly Quinn, Lecturer,
Teachers College, Columbia University

conversations of curriculum reform

Complicated Conversation

A Book Series of Curriculum Studies

William F. Pinar
General Editor

VOLUME 12

PETER LANG
New York • Washington, D.C./Baltimore • Bern
Frankfurt am Main • Berlin • Brussels • Vienna • Oxford

Kathryn M. Benson

conversations of curriculum reform

Students' and Teachers' Voices Interpreted Through Autobiographical and Phenomenological Texts

PETER LANG
New York • Washington, D.C./Baltimore • Bern
Frankfurt am Main • Berlin • Brussels • Vienna • Oxford

Library of Congress Cataloging-in-Publication Data

Benson, Kathryn M.
Conversations of curriculum reform: students' and teachers' voices interpreted through autobiographical and phenomenological texts / Kathryn M. Benson.
p. cm. — (Complicated conversation: a book series of curriculum studies; v. 12)
Includes bibliographical references and index.
1. Curriculum change. 2. Education, Secondary—Curricula—Philosophy.
3. Critical pedagogy. I. Title. II. Series: Complicated conversation; v. 12.
LB1628.B42 375'.006—dc22 2005035622
ISBN 0-8204-7479-7
ISSN 1534-2816

Bibliographic information published by **Die Deutsche Bibliothek**.
Die Deutsche Bibliothek lists this publication in the "Deutsche Nationalbibliografie"; detailed bibliographic data is available on the Internet at http://dnb.ddb.de/.

Cover design by Lisa Barfield

In memory of my mother & students

Contents

Preface: Willian E. Doll, Jr.

In one of his works (*Troubadour of Knowledge*), Michel Serres takes an ordinary incident—a left-handed school child—and turns it into a book describing not only teaching and learning but also life and loving. May I say that Kathryn Benson in her book (*Conversations of Curriculum Reform: Students' and Teacher's Voices*) has done much the same. The incident is simple, the material rich. In the early 1990s, Kathryn as teacher and researcher engaged a group of ninth grade students to discuss their reactions to the curriculum they had, the teachers who were teaching, the sense and meaning of learning to which they were exposed. A decade later, Kathryn and some of participants (now young adults) revisit the tapes of the conversations and the experiences they had. Interestingly, Kathryn's original intent to give the students' a recursive/reflective voice, looped back on itself and she found herself:

> In writing about my students, I looked on the scripted pages and found not just them but myself.... I am reflected in their writings as surely as if they held a mirror to my face.

Such recursion shocks Kathryn and she begins to wonder what it means to teach, to engage the other, to find self, indeed to live. Kathryn reminisces about her own journey from being a girl in a small, southern, segregated town to being a college student, teacher, and finally university professor/researcher.

Along this journey, written in a delightful and poetic manner, we come in contact with Kathryn coming in contact with racism, sexism, discrimination, death, poetry, critical theory, loneliness, a dawning intellectuality, maturity. In short, Kathryn's awareness of herself becomes our awareness of her and indeed of ourselves and of life itself. Kathryn uses autobiographical and phenomenological devices and reflections as she (and we) take this journey. We come in contact with some of the great intellects of the 20th century: Bakhtin, Derrida, Dewey, Gadamer, Habermas,

Heidegger, Husserl, Merleau-Ponty, Ricoeur, Rorty—all of whom she quotes liberally and well. Here is a panoply of stimulating quotes, provoking us to wonder about life, its meaning, and our place within life. The phenomenological experience of living is brought to our attention on page after page. The text here is most rich.

We are also introduced to current curricular theorists such as Aoki, Greene, Pinar, Van Manen (to name but a few) who ask us to reflect on what it means to educate in a climate in which education is replaced by the mimesis of schooling (to use Donna Trueit's felicitous phrase). We feel the contrast between the depth of thought in our past century's great philosophical and phenomenological thinkers and the shallowness of our current administration's views on learning and living. As depressing as this contrast is, it is enlightening. We see clearly what must be changed.

The book does not lead us to a dead end in its journey, though. As Kathryn talks with her original participants a decade after the first set of reflections, when they were ninth graders, she sees, that "curriculum is trumped by care" (106). There is an aliveness in youth, now as in the early 90s or the early 60s when Kathryn was a teenager. No matter how "dead," "lifeless," "dull" and "barren" (to use A.N. Whitehead's phraseology) the curriculum may be, life is still vibrant, dynamic. Youth are able to bring forth this vibrancy of life if we will but introduce care into our daily activities, or daily intercourse with our students. A curriculum may (regretfully) be "narrow and technocratic" (116), but life is not. To introduce care into the curriculum, care for self, for others, for the earth on which we live, and the air we breath, is now Kathryn's task. And a noble task it is.

As I finish this hopeful and care-filled book, I am reminded of the words of Michel Serres at the end of *Troubadour of Knowledge*:

> *Reborn, he knows, he takes pity.*
> *Finally, he can teach.*

—WM. DOLL, VIRA FRANKLIN AND J.R. EAGLES PROFESSOR, LOUISIANA STATE UNIVERSITY

Acknowledgments

My journey as a student of curriculum and curriculum theory began at Louisiana State University in Shreveport under the direction of Joe L. Kincheloe and Joe L. Green. Both of these astute professors guided my study of the history and philosophy of education in theoretical and pragmatic directions so that I returned to my own classroom geared and guided toward teaching in ways that students and teacher could actually live in the learning and love the lesson. I continue to thank them for the studies they made possible and for the spaces they made available for a teacher from a small school in north Louisiana to become a teacher/researcher/practitioner.

Continuing studies at Louisiana State University in Baton Rouge, I enjoyed the teachings of Bill Doll, Mary-Ellen Jacobs, Tony Whitson, and others whose voices joined mine in the celebration of curriculum. The graduate students there were an important part of the experience as we worked and talked and wrote our ways toward dissertations. Natalie Adams and Molly Quinn were great supports and friends during this time. Also, most importantly, my husband and three daughters were always encouraging and interested in my progress and were integral to my well-being.

The students at Springhill High School are the critical element in my work. The group of ninth graders with whom I researched for two years and who later continued the study as adults was essential and central to the project. Their efforts and care have sustained my work for years. The two that we lost during the second year have continued to be a presence in all of our lives. As instructed, we will not forget.

During the production of the book, my Southern Arkansas University family has been instrumental in the completion of the text. Gayle Coston, Donna McCloy, and Del Duke lent their technical expertise and encouragement. The SAU Faculty

Research Grant that I received made the book proposal possible and started the effort to complete the task of writing this book. Colleagues Kim Bloss, Denise Moseley, and Deebe Milford were always supportive and willing to listen to me as I talked my way through the chapters of the text. In the final stages of the project, graduate assistant Jason W. Clark assisted in numerous ways to make possible a final copy. His skills as editor were invaluable. I thank these SAU friends.

Finally, I must thank my mentor William F. Pinar, scholar exemplar. Reading, researching, and writing are my passion and Bill has certainly contributed to this effort. His steady willingness to advise and encourage have made this work possible. Thank you.

Thank you to the Harvard University Press, reprinted by permission of the publishers and the Trustees of Amherst College from *The Poems of Emily Dickinson*, Thomas H. Johnson, ed., Cambridge, Mass.: The Belknap Press of Harvard University Press.

Introduction

How do I begin to explain my desire, my wish, my drive to write about students' experiences of schooling? How do I comprehend or express the realization that in searching for others I find myself? The fear of writing and the distrust of language to convey meaning render me voiceless, speechless, wordless. How can I explain what I cannot understand? Where did I begin and where am I going? What does it mean to look backward and forward while in the quagmire of the present? How can I speak lucidly in the face of chaos? Does consciousness begin in inchoate chaos?

Must we structure and render all experience into reason and order? The Greeks taught that first there was only chaos from which came night and Erebus; miraculously, from darkness and annihilation came love. Only then could light appear. From nothingness came love. Pre-scientific minds could comprehend and move past the nothingness that plagues our communal consciousness. Not reason, but love illuminated our lives.

Love, the flesh, the body, the presence, the living warmth of other human beings—these are the physical possibilities that draw me to the classroom. I seek first the connections, the relationships, the communal and individual understandings that are made possible by the school setting and its attendant curricula of school subjects and myriad activities that pass as education.

Not only the body but also our language draws us close—through reading, speaking, listening, and writing. We speak ourselves into being. Often its power perversely throws us asunder and renders us voiceless. Sometimes we understand only in silence; indeed, sometimes the silence screams. Sometimes death resides in life, waiting to show himself and speak to us in stern, authoritative tones and pronounce himself the ultimate victor. He is rarely rational, but presences himself in unexpected and capricious manner.

The Focus

Curriculum has been studied extensively in its physical manifestations and all that entails—the downward look from Mt. Olympus to the rocky crags of school life. The students are seen scurrying as if in flight from winged predators determined to pick a tasty morsel of living flesh and devour it whole. Teachers huddle in protective and fearful enclaves of confusion and dismay. In so doing, the gap widens between the public and the private, the communal and the individual, the teacher and the student, teaching and learning, theory and practice, researcher and practitioner; indeed, it seems between chaos and love.

The hierarchy of non-inclusion, of dualisms, is artificially conceived and delivered as reality to our conscious practice. The students sit lifeless in their desks, tired recipients of pre-digested and mismatched collections of "inert knowledge" that lack the power to propel them into an upright stance of active intelligence and power(ful)-filled movement. The teachers move in rigid lockstep drills of curriculum guides and No Child Left Behind dictates. What does it mean to be a teacher? A student? What is curriculum? Where is the theory? Is it possible to teach or learn? Is education Socrates' truly impossible profession (Felman, 1987, p. 69)? What are the (im)possibilities of curriculum reform? What are the (im)possibilities of voicing these meanings?

Ways of Understanding: The Interpretive Focus of Phenomenology and Autobiographical Texts

Hearing van Manen's (1990) as well as Pinar's (2002) numerous calls for autobiographical phenomenological research into the lived experiences and relationships found in educational practice, I feel a strong desire to work toward an understanding of the existential relations experienced in pedagogical acts by the students who lived and learned in my classroom and by myself as a teacher in this classroom. I seek the interconnections and glidings between and in between theory and practice, the private and public, the political and social.

For Gadamer, understanding is a holistic process mediated by a complex framework and, also, an active process of encounter and response (Outhwaite, 1990, p. 27). In *Truth and Method* (1993) Gadamer speaks of the traditional conception of understanding as the process of operating within the hermeneutic circle in which we move back and forth between specific parts of the "text." Rejecting a stress on method, he claims that understanding is not a matter of trained, methodical, unprejudiced technique, but, rather, an encounter in the existentialist sense, a confrontation with something radically different from ourselves. Understanding comes when we are able to merge or "fuse our horizons" and "we must place ourselves in the other situation in order to understand it" (pp. 302–303). Of course, he is speaking of the historical horizon but extends the application to the personal. An added complication is that our horizon moves, of necessity, when we move. What a rich moment when we realize we are unbound by the present and are bound toward possibility. Such a "fusion of horizons" enables us to comprehend that the subject-object dualism that alienates and distances us from each other is perhaps the lack of an attempt to teach and reach those places where our lives intersect and intertwine or a failure to realize and (mis)understand those places where our lives cannot (inter)join.

Gadamer's and Ricoeur's moderate hermeneutics partially guide me through the interpretations of this study as I struggle to locate the prejudices of historical existence and the embedded limitations of language. History and language, ineluctable yet illusory. Accepting partial privilege to textual meaning, I yearn for the possibilities of communicative dialogue and conversation that allow brief and partial glimpses of inner being. If this is an impossible and romantic project, radical hermeneutics, inspired by Nietzsche and Heidegger and practiced by Derrida and Foucault, may allow for a reading of texts "more of a case of playing or dancing than a puritanical application of method" (Gallagher, 1992, p. 10). At any rate, truth is not the goal sighted by the fine hairs of an arrow but a wandering presence, a ghost, that beacons invitingly and then fades. One awakens to a sense of loss, a yearning heart that seeks to return to that place of light.

These thoughts lend themselves to the attempt to place my students, myself, my learning, my passion, my life, within the middle of a research project that attempts to locate those thoughts, feelings, experiences, desires, wishes, hopes that will lead us toward a connection of understanding, a horizon of being. How did I come to find myself a teacher in a secondary school, trying to teach students who presented a fecundity of (im)possibilities? What does it mean to be a teacher researcher? What does it mean to search my memory for whatever forces propelled me toward teacher education? In writing about my students, I looked on the scripted pages and found not just them, but myself. My initial attempt to allow for student voice made the spaces available for my own. I am reflected in their writings as surely as if they held a mirror to my face and sculpted my consciousness.

However, just as Ernst Mach (Hardy, 1987) discovered that perception is not an objective process explained by science, but primarily a form of subjective life in the world, I also find perception a problematic pose, an itching, driving, diving necessity to swim and navigate the murky waters of the underneath and filmy depths of schooling for my students and myself as we plunder and pick up those underlying bits of structures within our consciousness that frame our educational lives. We attempt to explore and explain and extrapolate our perceptions of schooling and curriculum in an exploration of how-school-is and thoughts of how-school-can-be.

The desire for school reform also fuels my work. Moving toward a reform effort that is centered around the thoughts and perceptions of students and teachers could lead toward schooling that is more than an effort to make a particular score on a standardized test or a pragmatic and technocratic effort to attempt to ensure that schools are not deemed "unacceptable," according to the guidelines of the current educational mandates of No Child Left Behind. These three strands of teacher voice, student voice, and school reform are woven throughout a two-year research project conducted in the early 90s and continued in recent years.

Knowledge Claims: Reforms Through Autobiographic Calibrations

We claim the authority of knowledge existing within and without our autobiographies, within our own lives and bodies, using the narrative and descriptive to express and explicate our everyday experiences. According to Grumet (in Pinar and Reynolds, 1992), exploring our own stories will place us face to face with our own contradictory experiences, thoughts, feelings, ideas. Grumet (1992) also writes that "If we must calibrate education, then we might say that we are educated to the extent that we are conscious of our experience and to the degree that we are freed by this knowledge to act in the world" (p. 33). We must indeed measure the worth of our educational lives, that measure of worth lying within our own experiences. Yet, I wonder how educators and others can assess such worth without seeking the meanings that the students themselves give to their experiences? How are teachers freed by a consciousness of their experiences to act as free agents in a school setting? Students?

To act in the world as active agent rather than as passive recipient should be a prime objective of radical education reform. Current educational trends are leading us farther away from rather than closer to a model of education that enables rather than cripples, teaches rather than dictates, empowers rather than indoctrinates. This project represents my entry into the complicated conversation to reform educational research and practice. According to Reynolds and Webber (2004), curriculum theorizing and research that is created and allowed to flow in Deleuze's "new lines of flight" will "dis/position curriculum research." Deleuze's philosophy of multiplicities makes epistemological, ontological, and axiological possibilities that are negated by, say, Plato's Idealism, Aristotle's Realism, or Rousseau's Naturalism. Complexities, complications, and complicities make authoritative control, a hierarchical institution less stable and more vulnerable to breakthroughs that challenge the "that-which-is" to "what-can-be" (Jipson & Paley as cited in Reynolds and Webber, 2004, p. 5).

At the beginning of this introduction, in response to the desire for "what-can-be," I spoke in the cadences of mythopoeic speech to delve and dive into the underpinnings of my interest in and desire to work with students and their experiences of curriculum and schooling, of my desire to understand self. This language pulls me closer than the dry, hard syllables of accepted academic discourse that bluntly states purposes, objectives, and aims, concluding with presupposed outcomes. It, rather, allows spaces for possibilities of multiple perspectives, meanings, and connections while circling and meandering recursively in a search for sites of understandings and connections of meanings in lived experiences. It guides rather than leads, suggests rather than exhorts, cares rather than knows. It leads in a quest for understanding of being rather than determination of absolute knowing. It circles in connections rather than separates in numerical spaces. It is a quest for reform that enables rather than cripples, develops rather than deforms, and empowers rather than totalizes. It is a personal quest for understanding of myself as a teacher and my students.

I (re)search myself. As I have worked back and forth through this text, I have lacked the ability to gain new understandings from my former students in recent meetings this past year. My intent was to re-study the original research findings, done with a group of high school students, with some of the participants. However, rather than reinterpreting, other than summarily, the conversations of the original study, I instead shifted my methodology to include autobiography. In complete frustration I looked inward. The focus rearranged itself from outward to inward. I shifted to the autobiographical, the personal, the pedagogy of my life. In the attempt to hear my students and allow spaces for their voices, my own surfaced and grew louder. I did not realize the existence of my own silences, the silences of my life, until I heard and explored theirs. Moving from a project that focused on student voice and schooling, I found myself in exploration of my own educational thoughts and experiences.

chapter **one**

WAYS OF UNDERSTANDING CURRICULUM AND SELF: AUTOBIOGRAPHICAL PHENOMENOLOGY

When I say, then, that these words emerge from suffering, I refer to that personal struggle to name that location from which I come to voice—that space of my theorizing.

—BELL HOOKS, 1990, P. 146

As I found my own voice in analysis, droning on day after day, it gradually took the place occupied for so long by the schools. One day it was inevitable that I should cease to be a schoolgirl.

—CATHERINE CLEMENT IN WALKERDINE, 1990, XI

Education is the point at which we decide whether we love the world enough to assume responsibility for it and by the same token to save it from that ruin which, except for renewal, except for the coming of the new and young, would be inevitable. And education, too, is where we decide whether we love our children enough not to expel them from our world and leave them to their own devices, nor to strike from their hands their choice of undertaking something new, something unforeseen by us, but to prepare them in advance for the task of renewing a common world.

—HANNAH ARENDT, 1961, P. 196

Elliot W. Eisner, in the introduction to Connelly and Clandinin's work (1988), writes that "One of the strongest aspects of *Teachers as Curriculum Planners* is the use of teacher narratives" (x). Never mind that narratives (the genre of Homer's oral epic the *Odyssey*; Fielding's novel *Tom Jones*; and Poe's *The Tell-Tale Heart*) for educational researchers are considered "soft data" that fail to inspire confidence in their reliability or validity or that these writings are bound by metaphor, "with individual cadences that convey personal meaning, and with those expressive features that do not lend themselves well to truth tests" (x). To the contrary, teacher narratives, according to Eisner, provide and convey meaning and, by so doing, provide ways to think about curriculum and teaching. The perils of the personal, the expectations from the stars, the fire lighting the sky, the imagining of the possible, the renewal of the young, all provide the desire for curriculum reform, a truer one that acknowledges the worth and value of the personal knowledge and lives of teacher and student.

Narratives of Self: Political Settings of Curriculum

Ivor F. Goodson in Pinar's *Curriculum: Toward New Identities* (1998) explores the intricacies of the current emphasis of the use of teachers' narratives of their personal lives in curriculum. This emphasis seemingly signals the value of their individual experiences, while ironically current curriculum policies and curriculum subject content are becoming more and more rigidly prescribed by political and social agencies. He writes, "In fact, at precisely the time the teacher's voice is being pursued and promoted, the teacher's work is being technized and narrowed" (p. 18). I am not sure that the teacher's work was ever anything but technical and narrow, to use a blunt axe, one dulled by my own twenty years of classroom teaching, but I understand the hesitation. He worries that "a primary reliance on narratives or life stories is likely to limit our capacity to understand social context and relationships as well as social and political purposes" (p. 10). However, I doubt that there will ever be "a primary reliance on narratives" and surely such a worry neglects to consider fully the context of the teacher's narrative that will ineluctably include the very elements he fears will be omitted.

It is a puzzling contradiction, contrariety, yet how do we story our lives without the details, influences, and results of the social and political contexts? What about the setting of the story? What about plot complications? What about thematization? Literary theory has long moved from New Criticism that limits the tale to the text and, instead, moves to give a panoramic view across boundaries of being to travel the social, economic, political, racial, and gender terrains and sites of contestation and negotiation. Is there anything but the text? Who is the author?

Kincheloe and Pinar (1991) write of the importance of place in understanding curriculum and schooling, "Indeed, place particularizes and conveys embedded social forces" (p. 4). The canon is contested in ways that are connected to these very social and political forces. Teacher narratives ineluctably include these areas in the telling of the tale, even if by conspicuously absenting themselves. Race, class, gender, the political all hover in the wings, if not playing central parts, rather like a pantomiming Greek chorus, wait to give context to the characters' sufferings and offer understanding of the drama's theme.

Indeed, Kincheloe (1998), in his explication of Slattery's *Curriculum Development in the Postmodern Era (1995)*, writes that the curriculum "is a holistic life experience, the journey of becoming a self-aware subject capable of shaping his or her life path" (p. 130). Not to negate or minimize the primacy or immediacy of the struggle for teachers and students with socio-political forces that dictate the regulations of school life, Kincheloe suggests that William F. Pinar's *currere* is always and foremost an unfinished product, always contingent on "the lived realities, socio-political encounters, and the identity formation of individual human beings." In contrast to Goodson's warning that the personal may obscure the professional aspects of teachers' lives, emphasis on the personal negates and neutralizes the academic tendency toward theorizing abstractly in Platonic metanarrative instead to include and recognize the lived realities of those around whom educational research whirls in patterns of (dis)organized research methodologies. Kincheloe also explicates Pinar's thought that "the discourses of social justice and individual justice as well as concerns with collectivity and individuality should not be in conflict" (p. 130). Of course we will argue against binary opposites and will embrace the notion that "For classroom teachers *currere* insisted that the self should never be collapsed into subject matter, that self and identity should be cultivated in relation to the learning process" (p. 130). Becoming researchers of self, our own subjectivities, we seek Kincheloe's "meta-dialogue, a constant conversation with self" (p. 132).

Conversations with Self: Personal Settings of Curriculum The Personal and Private (Dis)connections: Autobiographical Yearning

> Having the opportunity to talk about one's life, to give an account of it, to interpret it, is integral to leading that life rather than being led through it.... Part of human life, human living, is talking about it, and we can be sure that being silenced in one's account of one's life is a kind of amputation that signals oppression. Another reason for not divorcing life from the telling of it is that as humans our experiences are deeply influenced by what is said about them, by ourselves or powerful (as opposed to significant) others.... We can't separate our lives from the accounts given of them; the articulation of our experience is part of our experience.
>
> (Lugones, M.C., & Spelman, E.V., as cited in Rice and Burbules, 1993, p. 37)

I claim Gadamer's thought that "emancipation is attained in and through conversation (Gallagher, 1992, p. 289). Indeed the hope feeds my own need, my desire, my motivation, to connect, to belong, to escape the angst of individualism, in this troubled world of ours, despite knowing full well, and, indeed, having lived and suffered many failed attempts at connection, at understanding. I have not only lived failed relationships on all sorts of interpersonal levels, but also I have ironically and, I would argue, productively spent my life reading and re-reading literature in which and through which I lived the characters' failures and successes as they too attempted the naïve projects of connecting their lives to those of others and learning self. This is the linguistic project of hermeneutics.

As a college student, wandering the mostly deserted aisles of the library, as lonely as I on weekends, all deserted, I searched for something to fill the void of the sometimes shallow relationships of adolescence, to fill my mind, to seek for understanding of life and of myself. I realized at the time I was living my life on at least two levels, one playing the part of typical and stereotypical college student, boy-crazy and party-driven, the other playing/being an alternate me as I floundered toward a sense of self, an identity. Of course, I found Thomas Wolfe, William Faulkner, Sinclair Lewis, Theodore Dreiser, F. Scott Fitzgerald, American authors absent from the required readings for my mostly British literature classes; I certainly admired Wordsworth and Coleridge, conversed with bad boys Shelley and Byron. All male, all white, too, I remembered the names of American authors mentioned in my high school junior English literature book. Just as I had read my way through the Dewey Decimal system while working in the library during the summers of my high school years, I now sought to assuage my need to have something to think about with literature. I read the 800s. I read. I was a "reader, that is to say," according to de Castell's definition, "an occupant of literate space" (1999, p. 400). I read the texts; no one read me.

Thomas Wolfe in his work speaks of an incipient awareness of loneliness. For instance, in *Look Homeward, Angel* (1929/1970), the infant Eugene Gant, alone and bereft in his crib, ponders that "he knew he would always be the sad one: caged in that little round of skull ... Lost .... men were forever strangers to one another, that no one ever comes really to know any one...." (p. 35). Even more distressing and pertinent to this study are his comments that as he saw adult figures come and go from his cribb'd confinement, he intuited "that even their speech, their entire fluidity and ease of movement were but meager communicants of their thought or feeling, and served often not to promote understanding, but to deepen and widen strife, bitterness, and prejudice" (pp. 35–36). This truncated consideration of the angst of separation and loneliness begs for consolation. So, not only do we live in isolated individualism, but also we cannot trust speech to connect us to others in public or private ways, should we split or connect the two domains of ordering reality. O Lost.

Tellingly and ironically, Franzen (2002) writes in his essay "Imperial Bedroom" of the American mania for privacy, "a messy concept," he terms it, one that is legally unhinged from jurisdiction. Americans seem to be drowning in private details of the *other's* life while isolated within the narrow margins of their own private lives. The private is so public that the concept of public in which we connect in meaningful ways is obliterated through the violent imposition of its binary opposite. He claims that "What's threatened, then, isn't the private sphere. It's the public sphere" (p. 48). He cites numerous examples of the private, exclusive, isolated nature of our lives while we so rarely experience the public. To turn his thought toward the educational realm, we think of how schools, rather than shining as settings of public engagement with children's learning, sites of connections and relationships, instead have become part and parcel of the public's insatiable appetite, fostered by the media, for sensational and alarming details of failed educational reform, statistics of subgroups lacking required proficiency scores on standardized tests. The public sphere of education is gasping on the gallows of private opinion formed by the public media and bureaucratic agencies. With Wolfe and Franzen we worry the notions of private existence, public spheres, and educational reform.

In perhaps puerile longing, we consider Habermas's concept of speech that may allow for community connections; later we will analyze the (dis)allowances. According to Robert Young (1990), Habermas is insistent that it is in the presence of human speech that the possibility of freedom and respect for the potential contribution of each person to the total experience of humankind is evidenced. However, for Habermas, language is both vehicle of distortion (likewise for Wolfe) while, at the same time, possible site of truth. We speak in favor of the slight possibility, acknowledging the (in)evitability of the tentative (im)possibility.

I began teaching at a very young age, having graduated from college at twenty, but some years after Arendt published her work in 1961. In the early 70s, I was mesmerized, entranced by the students who came to my room, cardboard figures they seemed, expecting something, expecting that I would perform my role, perhaps hoping that the day would soon be over. Like Wolfe's Eugene, trapped within the confines of his crib and almost that desperate, I taught within the squared and isolated classroom, automatically, slowly, and numbly gaining expertise at lesson planning to capture the plethora and chaos of content swirling in my head, techniques to engage students as a way of classroom management, working with administrators and other teachers.

Slowly, the frozen, inert world of my childhood and teenage years thawed somehow and began to move in patterns of experience and thought, twirling toward awareness of myself and others. Love had always been a precious, scant commodity in my experience, my home, a tidy red brick box (I wrote a paper in a graduate English class once in which a professor insisted I omit these details), a minefield of subterranean depths of cold and distant madness with hints of possible violence. I am not sure what enabled me to become flesh and blood, unless it was the love I was later able to feel for my own children, my three daughters, full of beauty and joy, initially tiny forms of pink flesh, soft and yielding and responding to my tentative attempts to embody and express love. Perhaps that love transferred from home to school. At any rate, I slowly and painfully learned myself, becoming a living and breathing teacher.

Finally and slowly, I began to feel the warmth of love for Arendt's world enough to assume responsibility for it, though I lacked the words to express the emotion, maybe the consciousness to realize it. I, sometimes in partial and incomplete flashes of feeling, other times in full consciousness of the significance of the emotion, realized the value of each student who sat in my classroom and came to understand that the world would be shaped and shared by the same students that I taught. I learned to love my role as shaper of the future and sharer of a love of learning and knowledge. Unsurprisingly now the contours of Arendt's "common world" are even more difficult to trace in the outlines of this post 9/11 world that looms menacingly, full of fears and threats. The fear is cold. The threats make our hearts pound in constricting chests.

Narratives of Curriculum: Students' Experiences of Schooling

Nevertheless, though I then began to speak of my experiences as a teacher and the becoming and transforming meanings I found in teaching, those same students, "the new and young," sat silently framed by the contours of the square classroom. I had painfully and carefully learned to speak from the inner reaches of my being as a human being; could I stretch across the barriers to reach those I taught? While curriculum has been extensively studied in its physical manifestations, the students have been noticeably absent, according to Erickson and Shultz (1992). In writing a chapter for the *Handbook of Research on Curriculum*, they found that student experience of curriculum had not been of much interest to educators or researchers. "Neither in conceptual work, nor in empirical research, nor in the conventional wisdom and discourse of practice does the subjective experience of students as they are engaged in learning figure in any central way" (p. 466). Developing the notion that understanding of student experience has been considered incidental by researchers, teachers, and policy analysts, Erickson and Shultz found that the "moment-to-moment character of engaging the manifest curriculum" was understood the least by researchers, teachers, and students (p. 468).

Voiceless, silent, unpresent, passive, the students' perceptions and experiences of curriculum and schooling are non-presences in most current and past research. C.H. Edson (1990) informs that "researchers realize that what is intended by the curriculum is not necessarily what is internalized, yet they continue to devote their major attention to the physical manifestations of school curriculum rather than to how children actually experience curricula in wide variety and form" (p. 49). Clearly, the students' voices and viewpoints, "how students actually experience curricula," were not and are not considered primary data for educational research.

The "taken-for-granted," as presented by Schutz (1967, p. 74), seems to imply that no thoughtful reflection or descriptive analysis of students' lives within the school lifeworld seems necessary. This non-seeing of students leads to a paucity of understanding of how students experience their educational lives in school settings. However, Schutz (1967) reminds us that "a change of attention can transform something that is taken for granted into something problematical" (p. 74). Clearly, "a change of attention" is called for; research is needed that deals with the perceived experiences of students, especially adolescents (Brown, 1992; Kincheloe, 1991).

According to van Manen (1990, p. 183), the lived meanings of experiences are "the ways that a person experiences and understands his or her world as real and meaningful." In order to learn about these experiences, the lived meanings of students' worlds, should not the students speak to us as teachers, educators, and researchers about their school lives? The desire of a possibility that students act in the world as active agents and not, rather, exist in schools as passive recipients of state-mandated curricula and federally imposed reforms, encapsulated in teacher-proof teaching materials, should propel educators "to prepare them (the students) in advance for the task of renewing a common world" (Arendt, 1961, p. 196).

Knowledge with which students can willfully and purposefully create their own parts to play, write their own lines, surely will lead to a more satisfying and fulfilling scene and world. As we measure the worth of our educational system, practices, and research, we find that this quality, this worthiness, can be found or evidenced within the daily, lived experiences of the students. Van Manen (1984, p. 38) writes that "phenomenology does not offer us the possibility of effective theory with which we can now explain and/or control the world but rather it offers us the possibility of plausible insight which brings us in more direct contact with the world." Perhaps it is van Manen's "contact" that I find so attractive, the possibility of connecting somehow somewhere with others in communal learnings and livings. Brown (1992) asserts that, for van Manen, phenomenology as a "philosophy of action" is quite suited to a reform of educational practice.

Conversations of Curriculum: Autobiographical and Phenomenological Texts

The aubiographical writing of curriculum is, for purposes of theorizing, a close fit and necessary, essential, elemental aspect of writing curriculum phenomenologically.

Pinar's work in *Understanding Curriculum* (Pinar, Reynolds, Slattery, & Taubman, 2002) delineates three strands of scholarship regarding curriculum as autobiographical and biographical text: autobiographical theory and practice, feminist autobiography, and the last, in which I situate my writing, "efforts to understand teachers biographically and autobiographically … the 'personal practical knowledge' of teachers, teacher lore, and biographical studies of teachers' lives" (pp. 516–517). That I write about my students and my students write about themselves and their teachers goes without saying. I also locate these sites of curriculum theorizing within the first category which includes the "major concepts" of "*currere*, collaboration, voice, dialogue journals, place, postructuralist portraits of self and experience, and myth, dreams, and the imagination" (p. 516). This autobiographical, biographical, and hermeneutic interpretative stance that involves a "more direct contact" with the students' lifeworld and a turning to a realization of the significance of student perspectives to educational research and reform seems central to the formation of a pedagogy that is capable of the process of "renewal," of transformation, and of reform.

The starting point of the original research study, conducted in the early 90s, was van Manen's (1990) "empirical realm of everyday lived experience." This hermeneutic phenomenological inquiry was based on a series of curricular conversations and writings with a group of ninth grade students. Through group discussions and group interpretations of text created in reaction to lived experiences of schooling, the research participants and I attempted to make meanings and uncover the meanings of the structures of experiences of our school lives.

Through a series of dialogical writings and hermeneutic conversations, in the first research project, the research participants created texts and understandings through language that formulated incandescent, interrelated perceptions and understandings of schooling. However, we consider Derrida's concurrence with Rousseau that writing is a "dangerous means, a menacing aid, the critical response to a situation of distress" (1997/1967, p. 144). Speech is primary; writing a perhaps poor substitute. That our speech preceded our writing or complemented individual writings is, quite possibly, a strength of this project if we agree that this "exterior addition" or Derrida's *complement* is a substitution and only a "mediocre makeshift" for the face to face meetings we enjoyed in which the more natural moment of the speech act was the focus of and the purpose for our discussions.

As teacher and researcher, I attempted to draw closer to the students in a research group at a secondary school in order to understand their perceptions of curriculum, their experiences of schooling, their viewpoint of life. Indeed, my presence was an integral part of the project as I interacted with the study participants in curricular conversations and cooperative interpretations to uncover and reclaim our educational lives, though I can also claim that we (dis)covered and (dis)claimed nearly as much of our lives. Claiming an autobiographical methodology as useful to the project and framed by Pinar's *currere*, the movement from and through the "regressive," the "progressive," the "analytical," and the "synthetical" (Pinar, et al., 2002, pp. 520–521), I write of the past, look toward the future, consider the past and present, and finally "reenter(s) the lived present." As a phenomenological researcher, living my life as a teacher, woman, wife, mother, daughter, sister, existing within the boundaries of my own (auto)biography, I find that my perceptions and positions are an integral part of the phenomena being studied (Dean, 1982, p. 101). As Max van Manen (1990, p. 36) reminds us, "The aim of phenomenology is to transform lived experience into a textual expression of its essence." Still we created, edited, drafted, and revised our school text, parsing for meaning, explicating for expression.

In a recent attempt at rapprochement, we met, the participants, now young adults, to reconsider our work together, to reinterpret our findings, to remember losses, to record gains. We attempted to move our horizon from present to past, to look at the past in terms of the present, and to look at the present in terms of the past. What did we say? What did our conversations mean? How did we connect our experiences to curriculum and schooling? How do we now? Indeed, how do we know? Hoping to complicate and explicate ourselves by looking within ourselves and each other for meaning, we gathered. As we questioned the meanings of our experienced school lives, we discussed in group settings our writings and journal entries. Truly, as Gadamer (1993, p. 362) suggests, it is more difficult to ask questions than to answer. We commented on school happenings, joked lazily and laconically about the inane procedures we endured. Now listening to tape recordings for purposes of re-analysis, I am captivated at the ellipses, the gasps, the gaps in dialogue, the inconsistencies. Indeed, I wonder if some speech is deliberately elliptic. What did we mean? Is questioning an art? Can it be ciphered? Can it be classified, categorized, codified? What is Gadamer's "real dialogue" (1993, p. 367)? I cannot claim knowledge of the meanings we found in their earlier work as ninth graders.

The adults they had become had left the classroom and the world of adolescence and become conversant with conventionality, tradition, status. Indeed, they negated much of their earlier work and seemed to blame themselves for their thoughts about teachers, teaching, and learning. It was a curious thing. I try to understand. I turn to the methodology of interpretation. I cannot forget that the "renewal" of the young that will save us from "ruin" is a constant process of teaching and learning that leads toward the possibilities and varieties of transformation. Though we may dispute and trouble the progressive ideal of transformation and worry the notion of a curriculum that encompasses the possibilities of yesterday, today, and, perhaps, tomorrow, we search for meanings of curriculum that fly past the positivism of today's scientism and accountability confines.

chapter **two**

DIS/POSITIONING OF CURRICULUM DISCOURSE: TRANSFORMATIVE LINES OF HERMENEUTIC FLIGHT

"(F)ire moves upwards because it is at home there with the shining stars ... a stone falls because that is where all other stones are and it belongs there."

—Hans-Georg Gadamer, 1992

"Writing is dangerous from the moment that representation there claims to be presence and the sign of the thing itself."

—Jacques Derrida, 1997/1967

I ended the previous chapter with an admission of failure, a notation of zero. Recent attempts to reestablish lines of communication with the research group fell flat. We were falling stones. Congenial meetings and perusal of transcripts yielded curiously scant substance. Drafts sent via email were ignored. Communication faltered at the level of surface politeness. The moments of pedagogical engagement had passed into the distant past. There was no single view, no conclusion, just vagueness and inconclusiveness. The desire to understand more fully my position as teacher and the group's thoughts about their earlier work was perhaps a domination, an effort to gather data for interpretation, a simple-minded attempt to graze the surfaces of meaning without attempting to understand more fully their positions as adults, rather than as ninth graders. Time eluded us. There was not a reconnection or a continuation of the conversations we once had. Gadamer's "consciousness of the Thou" is a lengthy process, a complicated one that begs for proximity. My weak effort to reconnect with my research group to understand more fully our original work was wrecked by distance and time. Instead I now circle back to my understanding of the hermeneutical experience to reconsider pedagogy and practice, to reconsider my role as teacher and researcher, to map with a transparent marker my place in the world.

Consciousness of the Thou: Unfolding Layers of Understanding

Construing the highest type of hermeneutical experience as "the openness to tradition characteristic of historically effected consciousness" (1993, p. 361), Gadamer presents what he terms "a real analogue" of this hermeneutical experience in human relationships or in the I's experience of the Thou. Gadamer's stance is one that moves past communication as a means of simply understanding human nature as well as an experience of the Thou in which the drive to know and understand the person can lead to a position of domination. My stance is one that recognizes the importance of Gadamer's hermeneutical experience—"to experience the Thou truly as a Thou, not to overlook his claim but to let him really say something to us" (p. 361). My concern, in that original research project, was to listen in openness to what my students had to say. The difficulty lay in the translation, the interpretation of the spoken and the unspoken, the wandering and weaving of meanings that existed in, between, and beyond the sounds and silences.

Phenomenology calls for an active involvement in the pedagogical lives of students. As educators consider pedagogical practice from this closer, more physically present in the body, phenomenological perspective, an awareness develops of what might be for, what van Manen terms, the "Good" of the students. In discussing the concept of pedagogic good, van Manen refers to "the end … from which all our hope, love and inspiration for our children draws its meaning" (van Manen, 1982, p. 44). Tenderly, Aoki (1992), in his attempt "to unfold layers of understandings about teaching," thoughtfully listens to "layers of voices" that speak to us about what teaching is. He gives explanation of the scientific and technical understandings of teaching that seem to scream loudly today in this era of standards and bureaucratized reform that limits and maims students, teachers, and administrators. Then he turns his head to listen to teachers and students, in tune to a teacher's presence with children. He defines pedagogy, in the original Greek sense, as "leading children." He claims "Teaching is truly pedagogic if the leading grows out of this care that inevitably is filled with the good of care. Teaching, then, is a tactful leading that knows and follows the pedagogic good in a caring situation" (1992, p. 21). Our means and ends in education are to be informed by the affective, by the human love that Arendt would have us recognize and reach toward as an educational touchstone.

Lastly, according to van Manen (1990), phenomenology may be part of a philosophy of action in that it requires a sense of situated personalness. The required close engagement of the teacher and student that phenomenological research and practice require must lead the educator to a greater concern for that student. In discussing phenomenological research that begins in the lifeworld and brings to reflective and conscious awareness the nature of the events experienced in the natural attitude, van Manen (1990) posits the transformative ability of research that makes it possible that we "remake ourselves in the true sense of *Bildung* (education)" (p. 7). He cites Rorty's notion that "Hermeneutic phenomenological research edifies the personal insight" (p. 7). Concern, insight, transformation, remaking self seem to open possibilities for presencing Aoki's (1992) " pedagogic good in a caring situation."

Consciousness of the World: Unfolding Layers of Self

According to van Manen (1990), phenomenology, which posits an ontologically oriented methodology, provides, along with a deeper understanding of the lifeworld of the student, a more serious and thoughtful consideration of the world. Questions are raised about what it means to be-in-the-world. Phenomenology has as its aim "to raise what is implicit, tacit, non-thematic, and non-reflective into explicit, stated, thematic, and reflective consciousness" (Vandenberg, 1992, p. 121). To move from the unconscious to the conscious, from the unstated to the stated, from a passive accepting to an active questioning offers the possibilities of transformation and revitalization of life and fresh understanding of one's world.

Grumet (1992) writes that "for the phenomenologist, knowledge of the world requires knowledge of self-as- knower-of-the-world" (p. 30). Others (Clandinin, 1985; Greene, 1979; Noddings, 1984) have done theoretical work suggesting that teachers require a stronger understanding of the self in relationship to students, pedagogical practice, and curriculum. De Castell (1999) writes of teachers' interest in "building hearts and souls and character," while she terms "the formation of self as education's principle project" (pp. 399–400). Like her, I have lived my life, seeking my "place in the text." She worries the notion of liberatory practice in the classroom and complicates the position of teacher and student in unequal stances of power. Rather, she leans toward a more private reading of text and writing of self that protects the unprotected and serves the unserved. However, she still leads us toward learning self as constructing an avenue, a gateway, a means of possibilities of learning others. To learn self and others, in cooperative relationships, is to "enter a hermeneutic circle as conversational participants" (Hollingsworth, Dybdahl, & Minarik, 1993, p. 9).

Embedded within the original project to understand how the research participants and I perceived and understood our school lives was a desire to reclaim our shaky voices, to jar the silences, to stake a vocal territory, to be heard. As I stated earlier, I had not heard my own loud silences until I experienced the silences of the students. Indeed I seem to have lived my life in my own silences. However, another underlying possibility throughout this project was the active claiming of one's own experiences, the transformation from passive to active voice as recipients and makers of educational practices.

However, we remember Goodson's (1998) earlier part in the curricular conversation with wise warnings about the paradoxical nature of the call for "teacher voice" just as "the teacher's work is being technized and narrowed" (p. 18). Perhaps it is quite naïve to celebrate the personal or public at the expense of the social and political. Certainly it is shortsighted to highlight the personal while downplaying a critique of the social milieu in which the personal is performed. I think also of the literature pregnant with references to the "reflective practitioner"; even certain forms for student teacher evaluation call for reflection concerning student learning, teacher cooperation with parents and community, teacher collaboration with other teachers and administrators. Certainly a critical perspective is essential for understanding and promotion of the "good." This critical perspective allows for deconstruction of terms used in school programs for assessing student learning and teacher performance. Awareness of the subtleties of programmatic venues counteracts the totalization of concepts that are essential to "pedagogic good."

Self in the World: Mapping the Life History

However, van Manen (1990, p. 2) proposes that "the method one chooses ought to maintain a certain harmony with the deep interests that makes one an educator (a parent or teacher) in the first place." I search my own past to understand my desire to understand school experiences, my own as well as those of my students. I locate on the map of my life history the incipient beginnings of my desire to learn as a first grade student fascinated by the red and blue counting sticks during arithmetic, my first grade year nurtured by a beautiful, kind, and loving teacher, and that desire continues to flow through my life as I live the process of becoming a teacher mesmerized by the colorful and complex diversities of my students.

My role has been that of a lifelong participant as well as a constant observer of education. Schooling has always been what is most "real" in this world for me. School buildings, old and dusty, high-ceilinged with golden oak floors, windows soaring overhead; grassless, red-clay playgrounds with groves of smooth-branched crape myrtles; teachers, serene and menacing, caring and distant; school subjects and books, flat and multidimensioned, limiting and limitless. As such, this existential and autobiographical inquiry into the nature of lived school experiences is not marked with a predetermined beginning point and has not concluded at a set time (Darroch and Silvers, 1982). Indeed, I have enjoyed the fervent hope and possibility to continue this work, this hermeneutic conversation of school experience, toward developing a better understanding of students, their lives of schooling, my life as a teacher, and self-understanding, recent failures not a disappointment but an event in and of itself, significant in its lack of vitality and form.

After teaching Spanish and English in several public high schools for eight years, I began graduate work with the study of the foundations of education—history and philosophy of education. With each course of study and set of readings, I altered my ways of teaching students, of attempting to come to an understanding with them of the possibilities for learning and living. I also began to think in problematic terms of the ways of schooling, of the ways that I had been taught and of the ways that I was teaching my students, of the ways that they learned or did not learn, of the ways I lived my school life as a teacher in a school where little learning was expected to take place, where pep rallies were conducted in the teachers' lounge to celebrate dropouts of unsuccessful students. Who failed whom, I wondered? I felt myself a failure with each drop sheet I signed. I felt that I signed away their futures.

I came to realize at odd moments and in chance ways as I probed both my students and myself, through writing about and discussion of school matters, that I lacked an understanding of how my students experienced schooling and their lives within the classroom. I believe that I was "seeing" without "knowing" my students (Dean, 1982, p. 101). As mentioned earlier, Schutz (1967) maintains that "a change of attention can transform something that is taken for granted into something problematical" (p. 74). I gradually yielded; I turned to what kept calling for my attention and submitted to the demand for a deeper involvement with student understanding of schooling as I began my original research. Indeed, the research participants themselves were located at the center of the project and, as such, could not be distanced from any understandings that developed throughout the study. As a crucial part of the effort to reclaim, understand, and reflect upon how both they and I have experienced and are experiencing our school lives, we constructed and construed possible meanings from these lived experiences.

Like the ethnographer John van Maanen (1988), I oppose positivist thinking that is blind to the problematic relationship between the knower and the known. The subject-object dualism that makes possible the "disinterested gaze" directed toward human beings, placing them under the microscope of science, is untenable to me, perhaps immoral. Van Maanen adds emphasis to his denial of objective "science" by crying "a phenomenological war whoop declaring that there is no way of seeing, hearing, or representing the world of others that is absolutely, universally valid or correct" (p. 35). What we lack in certainty we make up for in depth of understanding. And do we need certainty to understand? What is certain? Of course this is a major problem of the Enlightenment, but we continue to labor under the delusion that there is a pre-existing reality about which we can labor to learn, quite the Augean stable. Where is the river Alpheus that will flush clean the quagmire of absolutes?

A pedagogically responsive project to develop an awareness of what it is like to "be-in-the-world" seems preferable to continuing the research and pedagogical practices of separating and alienating ourselves and our world by false objectification. As the hermeneutic conversation began, initial questions arose: What is it like to be a student at this school? What happens or does not happen in class while working? Who decides the content of a discussion or conducts the discussions? How does a student feel when in a classroom? What does the student add to the class proceedings? What can be learned? What does the student wish to do or say? The dichotomous realms of subjects and objects that depend upon each other for a meaning of existence need to be recognized and understood as interactive and continuous (Brown, 1992, pp. 48–50). Embedded and situated within the school setting, the research participants wrote and spoke of their experiences of curriculum and schooling. Now possibilities of spaces were cleared for students to speak, to think, to express their lives.

Beginnings of Silence: Consciousness of Life-in-the-World

I began my phenomenological inquiry "with silence" (Psathas, 1973), a careful listening that attempted to gain a more acute consciousness of the students and their educational experiences. Langeveld (1983) suggests that "As we all know, nothing is so silent as that which is self-evident. Thus it becomes our task to render audible, readable, articulate, that which is silent" (pp. 5–7). Perhaps this is a type of a positive silence, one welcomed and warmed by possible manifestations of speech.

Often, however, silences are unwanted, unwelcomed, unsolicited, undeserved presences in the lives of women, children, the poor, the disadvantaged. These are not silent by choice, by way of methodology, but are silenced by a society that is hierarchical in structure where many groups of people find themselves muted by dominant others. Tillie Olsen (1978) writes of different types of silences among different groups of people; she labels them "not natural silences, ... the unnatural thwarting of what struggles to come into being, but cannot" (p. xi). She begins a chapter with this warning: "Do not forget: The overwhelmingness of the dominant./The daily saturation. /Isolations./ The knife of the perfectionist attitude./ The insoluble./ Economic imperatives" (p. 256). How easy it has been for educational researchers to work in scientific paradigms of positivist research while neglecting to hear the voices of those in their research settings as they gathered and sifted data, evaluated, and drew conclusions to affect the lives of their subjects.

I turned to dialogical creation of text and conversation, interpretation through the hermeneutics of autobiographical phenomenology and intense listening, hoping to gain a deeper understanding of the multiple ways that the research participants interpreted their lives and constructed their brands of "reality." Again, I wished to listen to their voices and my own. In so doing, I enacted and lived an acknowledgment of the inherent worth of their experiences, knowledge, and lives. Also, the students themselves in the process of recapturing and rethinking their educational lives recovered at least some of the meanings of their "life-texts": past and present experiences bounded by the cultural, social, and historical boundaries of their lives.

An ontological rather than an epistemological basis for research placed this study within interpretative hermeneutic research which "emphasizes the discovery of meaning, its sources, and shared understandings, and potential for creating new 'existences'" (Darroch and Silvers, 1982, p. 101). This approach—phenomenological, hermeneutic, and language oriented—affords a pedagogy that is based on the careful and thoughtful consideration of lived experience (van Manen, 1990, p. 2). In order to see and understand the pedagogical implications of teacher and student interactions and school situations, a hermeneutic effort is made to interpret the phenomena of the lifeworld. A careful attending to language in writing and speaking, as used and lived by the students and teacher, is an integral part of the research process into the meanings of the life-texts of culture, society, and history that shape our existence and that are, in turn, shaped by our existence.

Interpreting Life-in-the-World: Reflective Recovery of Experiences

In the following sections that comprise this discussion of phenomenological recovery and reflective understanding of lived experience, I turn to a consideration of the following: the presence of the world as a pre-existing condition of life, Gadamer's hermeneutic circle as integral part of the process of understanding and his notion of the "fusion of horizons" wherein connections of possible and, for me, tentative understanding are conjoined, the dialectics of inter-experience which provide instances of tension between the surface features and underlying realities of experience: between the "taken-for-granted" and the "familiar-made-strange," a reflective attempt to re-consider and re-see the experiences of school life, and, finally, a consideration of research as a way of questioning the ways we experience and place ourselves in the world.

Within the framework of schooling and my classroom, the research participants and I attempted to understand the interconnections between and among our shared and individual lived experiences. In answering the question—What is phenomenology?—Merleau-Ponty (1962) tells that:

> Phenomenology is the study of essences; and according to it, all problems amount to finding definitions of essences; the essence of perception, or the essence of consciousness, for example. But phenomenology is also a philosophy which puts essences back into existence, and does not expect to arrive at an understanding of man and the world from any starting point other than that of their 'facticity'. It is a transcendental philosophy which places in abeyance the assertions arising out of the natural attitude, the better to understand them; but it is also a philosophy for which the world is always 'already there' before reflection begins—as an inalienable presence; and all of its efforts are concentrated upon re-achieving a direct and primitive contact with the world, and endowing that contact with a philosophical status. (p. vii)

This lengthy quote supports the notion that educational research should be centered in the lifeworld of the students, the "facticity" and concrete existence of the classroom that is shared by students and teacher. This "direct and primitive contact with the world" lends itself to recognizing the everyday, the mundane, the familiar that add up to the full significance of students' and teachers' lives. I add the significance of our shared lives as teacher and students live their educational experiences in interactive fashion. The world is already there before, during, and after the researcher completes her work in a school. Rather than looking at, peering into, probing at the educational experiences of students from a researcher's distant and "disinterested" gaze, our phenomenological research attempts to recover meanings and understand how they are connected to daily lives. Van Manen (1984, p. 38) writes that phenomenological research is "a heedful, mindful wondering about the project of life, of living, of what it means to live a life." This life is part of a world.

For Gadamer hermeneutic understanding is a holistic process mediated by a complex framework and, also, an active process of encounter and response (Outhwaite, 1990, p. 24). In *Truth and Method* (1993), Gadamer endorses the conception of understanding as the process of operating within the hermeneutic circle in which we move back and forth between the specific parts of the "text," or, in the instance of this study, back and forth between the varying forms of our daily lived lives at school (pp. 377–378). The students and I moved back and forth from the past to the present, from last year to this year, from yesterday to today. We were concerned with our relationships with teachers, family, and friends that were ongoing as well as past. Our life-texts of social, cultural, and historical components encompassed our total being and presented us with a wealth of experience.

Rejecting a stress on method, Gadamer also claims that understanding is not a matter of trained, methodical, unprejudiced technique, but an encounter in the existentialist sense, a confrontation with something that we perceive as "different" from ourselves. Maurice Roche (1973) posits the existential position as one which "helps us to see the ordinary as strange and in need of some explanation" (p. 27). An attempt was made to defamiliarize the familiar, to present afresh school experiences that seemed nonproblematic, nonimportant, nonunusual.

Understandings came when we were able to merge or, to use Gadamer's (1993) term, to "fuse our horizons" (p. 27). Gadamer writes that "The horizon is the range of vision that includes everything that can be seen from a particular vantage point" (p. 302). However, it is also possible to see beyond one's horizon. Such a fusion enabled us to comprehend that the subject-object dualism that alienated and distanced us from each other was the lack of effort or the feebleness *of* attempts to reach those places where our lives intersected and interacted to form new existences. Such a thought lent itself to the attempt to place myself and the research participants within the middle of the research project as we located those thoughts, feelings, experiences, desires, wishes, and hopes that led us toward a connection of understandings—a "fusion of horizons."

Not only were my students and I engaged in the process and project of (re)creating our educational lives, of (re)projecting ourselves into educational research, of (re)stating the importance of the daily lives of teachers and students, we also discovered in the process of dialogue a coming together of purpose and meaning. An additional subtext of our project was that of community. As well as speaking out to others in the research discourse and making a larger space for our voices to be heard in the educational realm, we learned to speak and listen to each other.

R.D. Laing (Dean, 1982, p. 102) proposes that existential phenomenology is a "process of coming to an understanding rather than a research methodology." Laing writes about the impossibility of understanding or knowing persons by studying them as objects: "A person is the me, or you, he or she, whereby an object is experienced." Only by referring to those actions experienced as beings-in-the-world, can one know oneself or others. Like many others who have worked to eliminate the dualisms from our thought systems (Dewey, Gadamer, Rorty), Laing maintains a interactive view of an individual and the world, realizing one cannot live without the world nor the world exist without the individual. Phenomenology, then, is a study of "inter-experience" in which the other person's behavior is my experience while my behavior is that person's experience. The relations between persons, the relations between my students and myself, are central to our understanding as we explore these experiences.

Just as students are unproblematically perceived as students in much research in the "taken-for-granted" status of technical rationality, a distinction can be made between the unheeding look at students and the look which seeks to pierce the surface of "facticity" or which seeks to peel away the layers of reality to the underlying substructures. The dialectical tension between the "taken-for-granted" and the "familiar-made-strange" provides the basis for a phenomenological understanding of what it is like to live the experiences of a student (Dean, 1982, p. 108). Phenomenology is considered to be an act of seeing, indeed, a training of the ability to see (Stroker, 1987, p. 18) in order to make the familiar "strange." The researcher's point of view toward this "seeing" is a reflective one. One must reflect upon, re-think, not only the seeing, but also the hearing, feeling, and caring in order to make the object of description, **the given** or *das Gegebene*, the lived experience of the research participant, into the subject of phenomenological description. Throughout this study, the research participants and I, in joint effort, aspired to see, to reflect upon the constant movements and shifts back and forth between curriculum, schooling, students, and teacher that always included our settings, our frameworks that were fashioned from all aspects of our culture and tradition.

These recursive movements provided rich moments of description as we searched for the dialectical tension of the "in between." There is a resistant tension between having knowledge from the "outside" and the "inside" (Dean, 1982, p. 74). Silvers (1982) points out "the dialectical nature of what is held by a person subjectively and what is held in cornmon intersubjectively in relation with others" (p. 232). Things, essences, events, movements collide when what is externally accepted is confronted with what exists within the human consciousness. Here we may trace the movements back and forth between the external happenings and internal perceptions of events and stop a moment when they transfix into an altered state of being, Gadamer's "fusion of horizons." Thus, we trace the outlines of the circles that shape the varying parameters of our lives.

The phenomenological understandings developed as we explored the depths of our perceptions of schooling. While it is possible to describe the physical characteristics of a school or a student, one cannot understand from a description of external factors what it means to attend a school, to move from class to class, to learn from different teachers, to study different subject matters. Ernst Mach (Stroker, 1987, p. 16) discovered that perception is not only an objective process that can be explained by the methods of science, but that perception is primarily a form of subjective life in the world. A primary aspect of this research project was to get beneath the surface features of schooling in order to perceive better those underlying structures within our consciousness and lived experiences that framed and helped make sense of our educational lives. Hardy (1987) suggests that, according to Husserl, the "appropriate way of working in this field is simply to 'see' what is going on in it" (p. 6). What Hardy labels "reflective seeing" peers beyond and underneath the straightforward and groundlevel perception of everyday experience toward a clarity of vision that sees things "just as they are."

Merleau-Ponty's teaching that we make sense of our experiences from within them leads us further toward reclaiming our educational lives. Our own perceptions organize behind our backs and without our permission. Merleau-Ponty (1964) writes: "Since it is from within the world that we perceive, our experience is always perspectival ... there is always more to the object than we can ever perceive" (p. xiii). To decipher our own (de)construction of meaning-making still claimed need of Husserl's "reflective seeing" even as we acknowledged Merleau-Ponty's "disorder and non-sense" (xiii).

Indeed, Grumet (1992) instructs us that our very inquiry into the nature of our lived experiences transforms them and that we must learn to deal with uncertainty and ambiguity (p. 31). Silvers (1982) informs us also that our sense-making will bump up against its outer limits and that we will "find things that we cannot understand" (p. 244). Through these descriptions of "the given," phenomenologists claim to give certain "explanations," though not causal ones. We described the given features of our school lives, went back to the experiences in recursive fashion in order to sift through them for meanings, for some grains of truth, for tiny breaks of light in the clouds, for one shining star in the firmament. We hoped that a look at the ordinariness of the familiar would enable us to "make strange" (Grumet, 1992, p. 37) the everyday in order to more perceptively pay attention to, give value to, and understand those things that make up our lives. Merleau-Ponty (1962) tells us:

> It is because we are through and through compounded of relationships with the world that for us the only way to become aware of the fact is to suspend the resultant activity, to refuse it our complicity (to look at it *ohne mitzumachen*, as Husserl often says), or yet again, to put it 'out of play.' Not because we reject the certainties of common sense and a natural attitude to things ... but because ... they are taken for granted, and go unnoticed, and because in order to arouse them and bring them to view, we have to suspend for a moment our recognition of them. (p. xiii)

The research participants and I allowed ourselves "to see," to reflect upon our experiences in order to develop a more acute self-consciousness of our lives and the meanings we gave to our experiences. Our point of view was a reflective one as we sought the meanings of our doing, seeing, hearing, speaking, learning, being (Stroker, 1987, p. 18). Like Sartre, "we would be stalkers of meaning" (Merleau-Ponty, 1964, ix). In so doing, we were enabled to make sense of our experiences from the situated center, from within our lives themselves.

Van Manen (1990) tells us that "From a phenomenological point of view, to do research is always to question the way we experience the world, to want to know the world in which we live as human beings" (p. 5). I am tempted to say that in order to know the world one must of necessity question the ways we experience the world. There are no answers to questions not asked. To research one must first seek the questions to ask. And one must want to know in order to question. Desire plays some part. Thus, the researcher questions through wanting. To want to know prompts and precedes the question.

Van Manen goes on to say that "to know the world" is "to be in the world"; thus, our research and our questions place us more fully in the world. He writes: "Phenomenology calls this inseparable connection to the world the principle of 'intentionality'" (p. 5). In *Experience and Education* (1938) John Dewey teaches "We always live at the time we live and not at some other time, and only by extracting at each present time the full meaning of each present experience are we prepared for doing the same thing in the future" (p. 51). We sought to become pedagogically attentive and caring to the moment, uniting ourselves to the significance of the details and dimensions of our everyday educational lives. We strove toward a thoughtful awareness "of the consequential in the inconsequential, the significant in the taken-for-granted" (van Manen, 1990, p. 8).

The silences we found were not always those superimposed upon our lives but, rather, those that are inevitable in the process of attempting to recover an understanding of our lives. The silence of shared understandings (Silvers, 1982, p. 233) framed our boundaries as we attempted to break through to deeper understandings. Caputo (1987) explores the notion that "Hermeneutics thus means both recovery and violence, both restoration and destruction" (p. 64). The retrieval of meaning that involves the clearing away of "the superficial and commonplace understanding of things which systematically obscures our view and subverts the understanding" (p. 64) calls for a gentle violence that carefully clears the deadwood of our existence. The "forceful setting free" of interpretation means swimming against the current, standing against a strong wind, and reinvigorating the terrible ennui that engulfs our everyday, ordinary lives.

I conclude this discussion by considering the questions that began my initial inquiry. But before the questions can come or make their presence known, the doubts and sense of not-knowing must be recognized. Gadamer's "logical structure of openness that characterizes hermeneutical consciousness" (1993, p. 362) leads the researcher to a fuller realization of the importance of the concept of the question. Long ago, I began to move toward a realization of Socratic *docta ignorantia.* As I worked with students and parented my children, indeed, as I walked in the world, I found myself in the midst of perhaps more nonunderstanding than understanding: the questions of life, the doubts of living, the indeterminacy of circumstances, the infirmities of spirit.

To narrow the focus of this educational exercise in questioning, I turned to the classroom and the group of research participants. "When a question arises, it breaks open the being of the object" (Gadamer, 1993, p. 362). The question is stated as such: What is it like to be a student at this particular school at this particular time? It seemed a simple enough question to ask. However, I suspected that the answers would be more complex and, as such, validate the worthiness of the question. Gadamer writes: "There is a profound recognition of the priority of the question in all knowledge and discourse that really reveals something of an object" (1993, p. 363). The revealing, recovering, and repositioning of the lived experiences of the research participants was the focus of the original research project. If, as Gadamer teaches, the art of questioning is at the same time the art of conducting a dialogue, then the hermeneutic conversations with my students through reading, writing, speaking, and listening (the common colors of the English classroom) filled the artist's palette with infinite possibilities of representation.

As I think of these conversations and consider the questions that were generated by our work together and the meanings we un/dis-covered, the underlying concepts of silence, voice, and experience floated to the surface of the texts of our lives. In the next chapter I attempt to weave these into the conversation as strands of meaning, as supports upon which we built our experiences together.

chapter **three**

SILENCE, SPEAKING, AND VOICE: RECOVERING CONVERSATIONS OF VOLITION

Voice promised presence, contact, and relations that would take place within range of another's hearing. And in that proximity the sound of the voice, the movement of breath, of teeth and tongue and lips carried the promise of speech.

—MADELINE GRUMET, 1990, P. 278

Language is not a neutral medium that passes freely and easily into the private property of the speaker's intentions; it is populated—overpopulated—with the intentions of others. Expropriating it, forcing it to submit to one's own intentions and accents, is a difficult and complicated process.

—MIKHAIL BAKHTIN, 1981, P. 294

To abandon crusading rhetoric and begin to think outside of a framework which sees the "Other" as the problem for which they are the solution is to shift the role of critical intellectuals from universalizing spokespersons to cultural workers who do what they can to lift the barriers which prevent people from speaking for themselves.

—PATTI LATHER, 1991, P. 47

Silencing, student voice, conversation, and experience are the touchstones that guided and formed my thinking as I worked with the research group. Each day as we dealt with different aspects of our learning lives, we attempted to break the years of stony silence, to speak to and with one another, and to more fully understand those events that had happened and were presently occurring in our school lives.

The classroom must become for each teacher and his or her students an alive place, a place where each moment counts for something, where each second is fully realized. The silences of frustration, isolation, and repression must be blown away by the winds of change, of renewal, of transformation. Rather the loud and gusty voices of vibrant students and teachers should echo throughout the long corridors and square classrooms of our public school buildings in celebrations of life and learning.

Teaching in the early 70s in a public, all-girls high school in a parish in the southernmost tip of Louisiana, I came in contact for the first time as either a student or a teacher with African-American students. I had lived my life as a white person in a white community with persons of color as invisible citizens of southern society. That this same society had a population of approximately fifty percent African Americans is puzzling and troubling and that I lived without consciousness of half of my town's population is unsettling and guilt-inducing. However, I entered the teaching profession after desegregation and quickly realized that half of my students were African Americans. The class roll contained their names as well as names of Cajun Americans with names of Gautreaux, Boudreaux, and so on. My study of the Spanish language and culture had made me aware of cultural possibilities. My parents' apparent lack of prejudice perhaps allowed for an accepting and open attitude to difference. My mother, as a young girl, was present at a public lynching of an African American man in the public square of a small Louisiana town in the late 20s. Her trauma survived for some seventy years in the telling. Her sense of justice was sharpened to a keen edge. For whatever psychical and psychological reasons, I developed as a young woman with open boundaries; a part of my personality refused to develop closure, sometimes a deficit, but in confronting difference or others, often an asset.

Entering my ninth grade English classroom, a student, crowned with a splendid puffy dome of carefully groomed and glistening hair and shod in platform shoes, would hesitantly approach and, after waiting to be noticed and greeted, would ask, moving lips hidden by a downcast head, "May I speak?" I continued to experience a *frisson*, a sense of slight shock at being asked to give permission for what I had always assumed to be a given right of any person, anytime, anywhere. Was I mistaken in my assumption that to live meant to speak? How naïve. Surely, I was, though I had no way of knowing that then. Could something as familiar as a student request become strange and unfamiliar?

At the same time, I did have some awareness of the subtleties of the question. The request exemplified the discourse of polite social intercourse at that time which taught that one did not speak until spoken to and one did not intrude upon an adult. Quite simply, a student did not interrupt a teacher. However, the repeatedly asked question prompted and urged an awareness of the underlying doubts and hesitations of one human being that another would and could allow her to speak. Not speaking, being silenced lay dormant in my thoughts for many years.

Silenced Voices: Culture, Society, and Politics

Why and how are people silenced? I think back to the norms of my childhood in a small, Southern town where the main industry was a single paper mill and a majority of the town's people worshipped at a Baptist church of some sort (Southern, North American, Missionary, Primitive). The politeness of Southern manners dictated demure answers while fixed gender roles demanded acquiescence. The religious structures undergirded a norm of absolute obedience.

Though this town has changed along with the larger American society, I find these memories yet valid and vivid as many groups in various positions of authority call for and demand a return to the values of the past, to the family and moral values of supposedly halcyon days of Edenic bliss and peacefulness. Recently, the political rhetoric of family values and patriotism is blended with a simplistic view of religion, one that is absolute and hegemonic which makes almost impossible or, at least, difficult the spiritual development we humans crave. That this skillfully developed rhetoric is forced upon an unwitting, for the most part, public seems unfortunate and dangerous for the continuation of a democratic society.

At any rate, that these former days of conservative society, these hours and days and years of my growing up in a strictly segregated society, have a dark underside has not been much discussed. I remember the tension and strict guidelines of those days. I suffered the silence of the home, church, and school. The repression of the fifties and sixties, the racial and gender inequities, the classrooms of absolute teacher authority, and the sounds of the fiery and furious and screaming preacher in the pulpit, live still in my mind and consciousness. Today this simplistic call for things that never actually were cause us all schizophrenic nightmares. I shudder.

Silence, not speaking, standing mute in the face of external authority. Who speaks? May we speak? Children are typically silenced in the home, in the church, in the school as their demands and questions rattle adult sensibilities and sanity. Often children who are abused feel that no one will hear their tales of fear and pain. Some have suppressed memories that lie inside wailing. Who can hear the silent cry? Adolescents smother their conflicting and raging emotions in the face of adult superiority and rationality. Some commit suicide. Many mothers sit quietly as the fathers make the decisions and plan the finances. The entire family is silenced in family worship on Sunday morning, in a visit to the family doctor, in a legal proceeding in a courtroom. Clearly and quite often, being silent is an admission of and a state of submission, inferiority, powerlessness, lack of knowledge.

What determines who will speak? If we are able to link being silenced to a lack of power, then we might subscribe the position of power to those systems that determine how we live our lives—political, religious, educational, and social. The hierarchy of power that dictates who will speak and who will be silenced ensures that the father who is the titular, if not *de facto*, head of the household will find his counterpart in the school administrator. In Western thought the God, who made man in his image and woman as an afterthought, from man's rib, and children, born in reddened agony, as the result of Adam's and Eve's sin, finds his fleshly representative in the church pastor or priest, the father in the home, and the school administrator (Grumet, 1988, p. 55). All impose order and rationality upon the chaos of life.

How may we in education hear the silenced and recognize the presence of what is not spoken or allowed to be voiced? Don Ihde (1976) proposes that "In everything 'said' there is the latent horizon of the 'unsaid' which situates the said" (p. 166). Actually the position of the "unsaid" locates firmly and locks in place that which is "said." Unfortunately, this makes it possible through what Ihde terms as "easy or naive listening" to overlook or forget what is not being said. The latent meaning of the horizon remains unrecognized and unattended. While he hardly is arguing for the decentering of the said, as I would like, Ihde does make the point that the spoken precludes that which is not spoken and that this not-spoken is easily ignored. We, speaker and listener alike, teacher and researcher, take for granted the privilege of the spoken utterances as being worthy of our entire attention and those who are allowed to speak as being worthy of voice. We do not hear the message of the "unsaid" or the silences nor listen to the silent.

In consideration of various groups of silenced peoples, Rice and Burbules (1992) report that in feminist scholarship the disenfranchisement of the poor, nonwhite, and women is frequently expressed in terms of "silence" (p. 36). Perceiving themselves as silenced by exclusion from conversations by the failure of more privileged participants to take seriously their perspectives, these groups sometimes withdraw from the discourse of communication, in self-imposed silencing. Perhaps for them silence is a negative form of resistance, but the price is high for us all.

Donna Trueit (2002, p. 274) adds to this discussion of silence as she writes "Silence is not simply the absence of speech: it signifies spaces, gaps, and discontinuities in conversation, which have significance in admitting the untidiness, complexities and resistances in real life." I think of the students, girls as well as boys, I have taught who sat in the back *or* even front of the classroom in perfect stillness and silence. Did they learn or did they and I allow their minds to be as still as their quiet shapes in the metal desks? How can a consideration of these "spaces, gaps, and discontinuities in conversation" speak to our understanding? Lugones and Spelman (1983, p. 573) stress the importance of speaking to human life in terms of domination: "Part of human life, human living, is talking about it, and we can be sure that being silenced in one's account of one's life is a kind of amputation that signals oppression." Perhaps silence signals oppression. Perhaps it signals away from itself toward a meaning or meanings that are submerged in the subtexts of experience.

Not only in the realm of feminist scholarship but also in the sphere of women's writing do we find that women have typically been refused the spaces to break the silences that bind their lives (Gilbert and Gubar, 1985). Also, Froula (1989) tells us that speaking before the London/National Society for Women's Service in 1931, Virginia Woolf compared the woman novelist to a fisherwoman who lets the hook of her imagination down into the depths "of the world that lies submerged in our unconscious being" (Woolf, 1978, pp. xxxviii–xxxix). Pulling up the violently jerking line, the woman finds the "imagination … in a state of fury." Responding to the imagination's claim of interference, the woman replies, "My dear you were going altogether too far. Men would be shocked." Woolf found that women were still not allowed to tell their stories and a silence was to be found within all the writing by women she knew, even her own. What is not said? What is said by being not-said? The dialectic of the said and unsaid moves toward a louder sound of oppression.

Within the classroom, the students of many teachers sit still and silent as statues. For some, silence is a weapon, a refusal to speak, a defense against the teacher who has all the "answers." For others, silence is an unwelcome guest who is refused a cordial host's greeting. In some classrooms, girls are made welcome to speak and feel free to enter into the classroom activities either by the teacher or by internal motivation or interest; in others, boys feel more comfortable in voicing opinions or offering answers to teacher prompts. The purpose of considering the problematics of silence is to make it appear as a component of classroom discourse and practice, to make the inaudible and invisible—audible and visible.

The traditionalists or reactionaries, for the most part white, male, and middle class, those whom this system has most benefited, speak in support of the reinforcement of a belief system that places them in positions of authoritative superiority. However, a clamoring to speak is now being heard in loud calls from groups of marginalized peoples—women, black and white; gays and lesbians; children of all shapes and sizes and ages; black men; immigrants; the elderly; and the poor. In short, all of those people who might very well have asked in days past—"May I speak?"—are now speaking.

The stories have begun to be told. Black women writers such as Maya Angelou with *I Know Why the Caged Bird Sings* (1969) and Alice Walker with *The Color Purple* (1985) are literary examples of breaking the code of silence, of resisting the barriers of noninclusion. Angelou broke her own silence brought about by child abuse by entering into a literary culture that actually excluded her experiences as a black female. Reciting Shakespeare's *Rape of Lucrece*, she subverted white culture and literary tradition by affecting her own escape through that which denied her culture and history. Alice Walker's *The Color Purple* portrays a cure of the daughter's hysterical silence while recreating and repositioning the cultural text that sanctions her violation and dictates her silence. Labeling her work an "historical novel," Walker lays the truth claims of history upon her own invention, one which challenges the foundations of "conventions," those social and cultural forces that mold a woman's silence. These forbidden stories allow others to follow and include themselves in the speaking of the "unsaid."

Claiming to be one of "those ... who would participate in the formation of counter-hegemonic cultural practice to identify the spaces where we begin process of re-vision," bell hooks (1990, p. 145) determines to resist the oppression formed by race, sex, and class domination. Her most important claim for this study, I feel, is one that she repeats often—"Language is also a place of struggle" (p. 145). We struggle to find the safe places to speak ourselves into existence through our language. Sometimes we speak where it is dangerous. Students struggle to find classrooms where they may break the codes of their silences to presence themselves through their language. They struggle to speak. Labeling her silences as "unaddressed places within personal, political, and artistic evolution," hooks stakes out the margins as her territory within which multiple voices are heard. "When I say, then, that these words emerge from suffering, I refer to that personal struggle to name that location from which I come to voice—that space of my theorizing" (p. 146). While for her the margins are both sites of repression as well as sites of resistance, she positions herself away from the reductionist category of "other." Finally, bell hooks writes that "We fear those who speak about us, who do not speak to and with us. We know what it is like to be silenced" (p. 151).

Similarly, Audre Lorde (1984) calls for the transformation of those places of silences into positions of re-vision, re-creation. Believing that what is most important to her must be spoken, she willingly takes the risk of being misconstrued or misunderstood (p. 40). In discussing her bout with cancer, she writes that "Death ... is the final silence" (p. 41). Yet what she regrets most were her silences, silences that lacked any power, even the power to protect her. She calls for the transformation of silence into language and action.

According to Valerie Walkerdine (1990), feminism has concentrated on "finding a voice," providing both a place and power to speak. Silence as repression and resistance represents itself as either "presence or absence, a suppression versus an enabling" (p. 31). Like Audre Lorde, who calls for the transformation of silence into active language, Walkerdine states that what is important is "what can be spoken, how and in what circumstances" (p. 31). Attending to what is left out in the speaking and "how particular forms of language, supporting particular notions of truth, come to be produced" (p. 31) structure a framework for determining how speaking and silence, even the production of language itself, are fashioned into objects of regulation. Walkerdine realizes that we must and do struggle to break free but she asks a crucial question—"but to what?" (p. xiii).

"As I found my own voice in analysis, droning on day after day, it gradually took the place occupied for so long by the schools. One day it was inevitable that

I should cease to be a schoolgirl" (Catherine Clement qted in Walkerdine, 1990, p. xi). Rejecting the notion of an essential feminine voice, Walkerdine writes in the preface of her work *Schoolqirl Fictions* (1990) that one's voice is located in the interstices of subjugation. Here are found the other stories, some frightening and violent. The silences of children (especially girls) signal not a lack of thought or emotion or feeling but, rather, a lack of trust in school as a safe place to "speak" (p. 1). Where is it safe to speak?

Who asks the student to speak? When? Under what circumstances? About what? How often? Any school corridor, walkway, cafeteria, parking lot is suffused with sounds. Students talk, shout, whisper, laugh, push, shove, hug, shuffle, run, hustle into classrooms with sounds streaming from them. Echoes of life fade as papers rustle, books fall, feet find positions, arms fold into place. Boys and girls are shrouded by the mantle of the quiet routine of classroom practices. Where are the sounds? Who now speaks?

Jerome A. Popp (1987) writes that "Educational administrators value silence, and the teachers who must answer to them have devised ways to achieve it" (p. 145). My own daughter, a neophyte teacher, calls me daily with a report of her tiny first graders. Her telephone litany includes narrative and descriptive details of the principal coming in on errands and her concern that her students are not too loud while they color or make family figures (of mommy and daddy) with construction paper in his presence, not an observation visit, but a casual one. I cannot burden her yet with my stance that yearns for movement and noise, for talk and interaction. I nod silently while we talk on the telephone and suggest that she play music while they work and then promise that they will sing the songs when they finish their activities or talk about their doings when finished. I try to negotiate among school dictates (the hidden curriculum), her inexperience, and the yearnings of my heart.

Since silence for many educational administrators is a signal for learning, at least a prerequisite; it seems "natural" as well as essential to them that the classroom be a model of tranquility as the students work quietly with heads bent over their books or listen attentively as the teacher lectures. The structure is in place: the students listen to the teacher who listens to the principal/administrator who listens to the district superintendent. Of course, this simple sketch goes much further and is more complicated. On the one hand, silence equals learning; on the other, it indicates docility, passivity, receptivity. The dominant social structures stay in place. My daughter's first graders, tiny children who cannot read or write, have to be quiet while they color and cut.

Michelle Fine (1987) begins her article "Silencing in Public Schools" with a quote from Adrienne Rich: "Lying is done with words and also with silence" (p. 157). Fine problematizes the issue of silence by defining it as constituting "a process of institutionalized policies and practices which obscure the very social, economic, and therefore experiential conditions of students' daily lives, and which expel from written, oral, and nonverbal expression substantive and critical 'talk' about these conditions" (p. 157). After all, if one talks, one talks about some **thing**—an unfair statement made by someone, an unkind remark made in jest, a way to do school better, a plan to help a student succeed, a wish, a sigh, a desire, an expectation from the stars, an expression of being.

Not simply a matter of a teacher's positive evaluation by a supervisor nor a student's passive ingesting of already digested, teacher-taught material, silencing insures that the system which purports to be a medium of mobility for students is neither critiqued for contradictory results nor reformed for learning which emancipates rather than imprisons or expels. Ignored are the economic, social, and educational institutions that structure class, race, and gender hierarchies that position the student as object within a predetermined slot/slice of life. Equally ignored as irrelevant are the lived experiences of the students—the passions, fears, desires, concerns, imaginations, dreams—that link them to their own biographies and communities.

Michelle Fine's works (1987, 1991) are among the scarce examples of research that attempt to free the student voice, to release from silence the concerns of actual students. Erickson and Shultz (1992, p. 480) concur with Edson (1990), Kincheloe (1991) and Brown (1992) that absent from most recent research is "the first-person voice of the student." Labeling such an absence of student experience from the current educational discourse "a consequence of a systematic silencing of the student voice" (p. 481), they claim that student experience is silent in research for ideological reasons.

Calling what is experienced by most in the classroom "a monologue followed by a test" (p. 481), Erickson and Shultz cite the absence of conversation in the ways that most teachers teach which precludes the opportunity for students to develop their own voices—"a critical awareness of their own ends, means, and capabilities in learning" (p. 481). I would argue that the teachers silence themselves, as well, by teaching their subject content in a nontheoretical, ahistorical, and noncontextualized manner. They cannot speak themselves while, at the same time, voicing, miming, pantomiming the mandated curricula. The *other* speaks, not the teacher, certainly not the students.

Revitalizing Speech and Presence: Reclaiming of Voice

Of what importance is the concern that speaking, the inability of some groups of people, students among them, be problematized in educational research and practice? Perhaps I search for some vitality, a revitalization of student presence in the classroom, a reclaiming of authentic life, a reform of curriculum, a path to self. Speaking is important on several levels and in various ways. From birth to death, an individual speaks his or her presence in the world. Speaking oneself into life seems an ineluctable essence of existence.

If speaking is of primary importance in the life of an individual, it seems logical that such importance be recognized within the school classroom. My own past experiences in school and my observation of my own and other teachers' classroom practices bear out the notion that student voice in the everyday, actual classroom is submerged in the daily grind of teacher-teaching, in the myriad processes of the school day.

Martin Heidegger (1973, 1993) presents the act of speaking as one that is elemental to our existence as human beings:

> The capacity to speak distinguishes the human being as a human being. Such a distinguishing mark bears in itself the very design of the human essence. Man would not be man if it were denied him to speak—ceaselessly, ubiquitously, with respect to all things ... the essence of man consists in language. (pp. 397–398)

To speak is to break the silence that separates one from existence. The baby babbles, the young child asks, the adolescent tells, the adult questions, the elderly remember—through speech acts that rely on spoken and other types of language.

Hannah Arendt (1958) presents Aristotle's famous definition of man (woman) as a *zoon logon ekhon* or a living being capable of speech:

> And whatever men (*women*) do or know or experience can make sense only to the extent that it can be spoken about ... Men in the plural, that is, men in so far as they live and move and act in the world, can experience meaningfulness only because they can talk with and make sense to each other and to themselves. (p. 4, emphasis added)

She strengthens her position regarding the importance of speech, as well as action, by arguing that through speech and action we place ourselves in the world, "a second birth." Not only do we speak ourselves into existence but we also act ourselves into the world among other human beings. She goes on to say that action and speech are inextricably and primordially linked because only through access to both can we answer the questions asked of each of us: "Who are you?" "What are you doing?" "What do you desire?"

Jurgen Habermas (1970, 1974, 1984), like most of the Frankfurt School, views the modern world as a place where most people have little control over decisions that crucially affect their lives (Gibson, 1986, p. 34). Habermas takes as his project the endeavor to work out a critical theory of society that will enable emancipation. One of the crucial components of his thought is his theory of communication or speech. According to Robert Young (1990), Habermas is insistent that it is in the presence of human speech that the possibility of freedom and respect for the potential contribution of each person to the total experience of humankind is evidenced.

Yet, for Habermas, language is the vehicle of distortion while, at the same time, the possible site of truth. Within the notion of the ideal speech situation is the inherent claim of emancipation. To recognize distortions, we must also be able to ferret out the non-distorted communication which presupposes truth. The four validity claims of intelligibility, truth, sincerity, and equal access to the process of assertion, questioning, and discussion open the possibility for freedom from domination (Gibson, 1986, p. 39).

Whether or not the ideal of Habermas's speech situation is or can be realized, his insistence upon the possibility of distortion-free communication focuses our attention on the unequal relationships of communication and continues the search for possibilities of voicing/speaking one's own existence. The kind of open discourse that is public and open makes possible the critical evaluation of the life-world of students and teachers (Young, 1990, p. 30).

We must speak and act to proclaim ourselves as actors in the world and to do so is not a simple matter of our own will and desire to voice our thoughts, emotions, fantasies, struggles, dreams. If language is a place of struggle, as bell hooks asserts, then we must problematize the spaces and sites of speaking and non-speaking, voice and silence, action and passivity. For many critical educators, the concept of voice constitutes the focal point for a theory of teaching and learning that provides for the possibility of emancipatory and radical reform. Voice includes the notion of open and free dialogue as well as critique and examination of one's own life situation which include those factors—class, culture, race, and gender—that shape the lifeworld (Giroux and McLaren, 1986).

Students and teachers attempt to make themselves "heard," indeed, to hear their own voices spoken aloud, and to position themselves as active meaning makers and doers. Mikhail Bakhtin (1981) defines the practice of voicing one's presence in the world as "retelling a story in one's own words" (Giroux and McLaren, 1986, p. 235). One's life is reclaimed; one's existence is proclaimed. However, there are difficulties to consider. Walkerdine (1990) and Grumet (1990) help us think about some of these difficulties.

For instance, Valerie Walkerdine (1990) would have us be conscious not of just the fact that we may reclaim our "voices," but that we must critically examine the content of our speaking and interrogate the purposes of our speaking, that we creep between and among the interstices of our quiet and desperate spaces of subjugation. One's own voice may possibly be interrogated and found to be not a single, unitary sounding out of a single purpose but a contradictory and complex mixture of polyvocalities. Who is speaking? How many speak?

Grumet (1990) worries the concept of *voice* as she speaks of her work in the academy, a mostly male academy, where her voice is in counterposition to the male text. She writes, "Voice promised presence, contact, and relations that would take place within range of another's hearing. And in that proximity the sound of the voice, the movement of breath, of teeth and tongue and lips carried the promise of speech" (p. 278). Yes, she claims that voice "splinters the voice of an androgynous speaker," once we distinguish the female voice from that of the male. Yet, she finds that the female voice, deemed inferior as it is linked to "narrative or autobiographical voices in educational discourse" that we may "petition(s) phallocentric discourse but ... not challenge its control" (p. 279). Yet, she calls for her own polyvocalities, "the chorus that is our own voice." This single voice is a triad of "situation" that "acknowledges that we tell our story as a speech event" that interacts with "the social, cultural and political relations in and to which we speak"; the "narrative" that "invites all the specificity, presence and power that the symbolic and semiotic registers of our speaking can provide"; and the "interpretation," that "provides another voice, a reflexive and more distant one" (p. 280). She goes on to say that all three parts of this voice speak as one person and provide a forum for the others. Calling her conceptualization "a dynamic, reflective, and finally collaborative version of voice," she stresses the importance of teacher empowerment and school-based management that will lead to better ways of schooling.

As teachers and students learn to speak in conscious fashion from their situated positions within the lived frameworks of cultural, social, racial, and gender sites, multiple and contradictory voices are to be heard within each shared speaking. These voices are explored as voice itself becomes the terrain of "interrogation and struggle in which knowledge and power and subjectivity and desire provide the basis for analyzing how particular contradictory discourses and subjectivities are developed, regulated, and challenged ... " (Giroux, 1988). Rather than a romantic celebration or shallow sharing of inner thought or narcissistic exploration of one's past experiences, this critical look at and listening to one's own voice and those of others uncover ways that the school, teacher, and student are embedded within certain educational and social forms or discourse.

Voice and being, voice and struggle, voice and uncovering of buried subjectivities, voice and recovery of power—power to recover, to know, to understand, to transform. If we can speak ourselves into being, then a recovery of those experiences that shape our lives can become the spaces, the tensions, and the possibilities for a struggle with teaching, learning, curriculum, schooling—those day-to-day happenings that form our school lives.

Giroux (1988) asserts that "discourse is both medium and product of power" (p. 116). Mikhail Bakhtin (1981) is worth quoting at length here:

> Language is not a neutral medium that passes freely and easily into the private property of the speaker's intentions; it is populated—overpopulated—with the intentions of others. Expropriating it, forcing it to submit to one's own intentions and accents, is a difficult and complicated process. (p. 294)

We find that voice is shaped by the frameworks of our lived experiences, that we must struggle to locate and speak that voice, that to do so is difficult due to the strictures and structures of our life systems, that power is an integral force in determining who is allowed to speak, and even the act of speaking involves struggling with ideological and material forces that we find ourselves involuntarily giving voice to, even as we speak.

Ideology is inescapably inscribed in forms of educational discourses (school board policies, parish handbooks, curriculum guides, evaluation forms) through which school experience and practices are ordered and constituted (Giroux, 1988). In recovering and respeaking our lived positionalities in our educational experiences, we find it necessary to account for the ways in which language, ideology, history, and experience meld to produce, define, and constrain/construct forms of teacher-student interactions and practices. Again, we find a "polyphony of voices" which are mediated within various layers of reality shaped through an interaction of dominant and subordinate power forms (Giroux, 1988).

"Language is a place of struggle"—the thought places my project and work at least partially within the framework of critical emancipatory and radical education. To struggle to reclaim voice and to attempt to resituate the student within the center of educational research and thought indicate a belief in ameliorative reform. So be it. One must hope and find strength to move toward better things, possibly a more democratic school setting or a more caring and nurturing educational system.

However, I must agree with some of critical pedagogy's detractors who, fittingly enough, claim that the issues of multiculturalism and racism are not specifically addressed nor the ecological crisis acknowledged adequately (Pinar and Bowers, 1992). Other claims are made that must be considered as critical pedagogy evolves and develops within the classroom. Like any other project, critical pedagogy may be misapplied and misappropriated by educators who assume that their own "voices" are to be louder than those of their students'. One must be careful in the speaking of one's words; speaking always involves listening to others. One's own active "doing" must not necessitate the "undoing" of someone else. One's position must not lead to the "nonpositioning" of another.

Speaking of domination, Patti Lather (1991) provides a helpful discussion of the discourses of emancipatory education within the frameworks of various feminisms and postmodernism. She writes that "Feminism displaces the articulation of postmodernism from the site of the fathers and opens up the possibility of a heteroglot articulation premised on multiplicities and particularities" (p. 27). Multiple possibilities and multiple voices enlarge the spaces where contradictory sayings and doings are allowed, acknowledged, and accepted.

While Ellsworth (1989) turns Critical Theory's basic questions upon its own premises and structures by asking and problematizing the questions—"which interpretations and 'sensemaking' do these discourses facilitate, which do they silence and marginalize, and what interests do they appear to serve?" (p. 298)—, she also problematizes the concept of voice. Like Mimi Orner (1992), who fears that student voice is an oppressive construct that possibly "perpetuates relations of domination in the name of liberation" (p. 75), Ellsworth stresses the "contradictory and partial nature of all voices" (1989, p. 312). Thus, Ellsworth lays the groundwork for the realization of multiple voices and subjectivities not only within the speaking subject but also within the listening participants in the project labeled emancipatory pedagogy.

My perspective as researcher who worked with a group of students who struggled to express their lived school experiences is one that recognizes that our understandings are tentative, always inconclusive, and contingent on the context of the school setting. The move toward self-critique can only advance and inform the emancipatory project. We can follow John Dewey's (1938) advice as he argues: "For any theory and set of practices is dogmatic which is not based upon critical examination of its own underlying principles" (p. 22).

Patti Lather (1991) would have us work toward making it possible for people to speak in their own voices:

> To abandon crusading rhetoric and begin to think outside of a framework which sees the "Other" as the problem for which they are the solution is to shift the role of critical intellectuals from universalizing spokespersons to cultural workers who do what they can to lift the barriers which prevent people from speaking for themselves. (p. 47)

To move constantly back and forth between one's own underlying suppositions which frame one's view of reality and the world to listening to those who constitute the lived world of others is to become knowledgeable about what it means to be a speaking and doing person, an active participant in society. To delve into one's own contradictions and competing voices is to listen to one's own voice. To hear someone else's voice and acknowledge the difference that this hearing makes in one's own perceptions and experiences is to become a different person, to grow, and to live.

Reclaiming Joyful Voice: Playful Conversations of Experience

Just as voice and its attendant silence and sister "unsaid" are crucial aspects of this research project, conversation becomes an integral part and focus of the attempt to reclaim student and teacher voice and express a tentative understanding of school experiences as (non)perceived by all. As the research participants and I spoke our presence in the classroom, we communicated through conversation. Through shared writings and discussion, we entered into the discourse of lived experience. The dialogue that evolved brought us closer to reclaiming our school lives. The conversations that we shared were the concrete examples of our lives. We, my students and I, spoke ourselves present through our conversation, through our shared experiences of language.

In *Being and Time* Martin Heidegger (1973/1993) emphasized the primary importance of discourse or talk for language. Krell claims that "Early and late, Heidegger remained on the trail of language" (p. 394). The act of listening, the silence that allows us to hear, is of equal importance to speaking. According to Heidegger, spoken words take precedence over weakened and diluted written marks, lying flaccid on a printed page. Finally, Heidegger makes the important claim that language has the task of saying something to someone about something.

"To speech belong the speakers, but not as cause to effect. Rather, in speech the speakers have their presencing," writes Heidegger (1973/1993, p. 406). In speaking together, we "say something about something" (p. 409). We address the things in the world, pointing to them and proving their importance to us. Through the telling, showing, and pointing, our speech allows the world to appear, to presence itself and our presence in this world becomes more real in the telling.

Hans-Georg Gadarner claims to be a "speaker, a lecturer" (1992, p. 64). Always behind writing is the speaking voice. Not that we can ever claim to exhaust the possibilities of everything that we mean or know or even those (im)possibilities of expressive language. We recognize our linguistic limits. Yet, just as hermeneutics allows things to "speak which come to us in a fixed, petrified form, that of the text" (p. 65), our language speaks and, more importantly, says something to someone.

Conversation, shared communication, is for some the essence of language (Gadamer, 1993, p. 368). Again, Gadamer proposes as a prerequisite of conversation the concept of trust or "good will" (1992, p. 71). Those who are speaking must trust that language can allow communication and understanding. Gadamer (1992) writes: "Social life depends on our acceptance of everyday speech as trustworthy" (p. 71). I would argue that the conversations or shared communication of students also must be regarded as "trustworthy," as for too long educators and researchers have kept actual student talk at a distance, preferring supposedly more scientific models of research to speak for themselves and the students. Yet it is perhaps within the conversations of students and teachers that the energizing processes of teaching and learning, knowing and doing, thinking and feeling come alive. However, trustworthy speech, a naïve expectation in our society, may or may not be present in spoken expression. If we take this thought to its logical extreme and worry the notion that some speech is not trustworthy, and if a viable social life is dependent on the presence of trustworthiness, perhaps we can determine one factor in the breakdown of our society.

Trying to stride the gap between Gadamer's hermeneutics of trust and Derrida's hermeneutics of suspicion without toppling is a disconcerting and uncomfortable position, but one upon which I choose to balance. And I, afraid of heights, can barely breathe in the rarified air of possibility. After all, if we can attempt to

> keep the trembling and endless mirror–play of signs and texts in play, to see to it that metaphysics does not have its way with texts—by arresting the play, recentering the system, stabilizing the flux, breaking the code, reintroducing the nostalgic longing for the origin (Caputo, 1987, p. 118),

we can act upon the notion that there is "nothing original to interpret" which releases us from the snared writing and reading which we constantly struggle to untangle with great sighings of exertion. This "innocence of becoming" is a joyful place of connection between "home and exile" (118).

Linge (1976, p. xi) sees the task of philosophical hermeneutics as being one that is ontological rather than methodological in nature. To be searched for and uncovered are the conditions that make possible understanding whether in conversation, experiencing a work of art, or even considering an historical action. The familiar world in which we stand and that unfamiliar one of another person, work of art, or world event are to be bridged by a process, a fusion of horizons, that has much in common with a dialogue between persons.

The hermeneutical conversation between a person and a text is likened to an actual speech exchange between individuals. Assumed are that both conversational partners are concerned with the same subject matter, that each opens herself up to the other by listening to and considering what is said. The common question or common concern of the partners in the conversation is the focus of the conversation as each person addresses the particular issue. Just as the common question for this research project—What is it like to be a student at this particular school?—guided our conversation, so too does the openness of the question lead a conversation. Later, our conversation turned to the more serious discussion of what is it like to lose two friends in a car accident. Guided by exigencies of experience, we turned to the immediate topic. The familiar world of school and home became the unfamiliar one of loss and pain.

Language becomes the medium of understanding. Understanding leads to further discussion in an infinite interplay between the said and unsaid as new thoughts evolve. We are held captive by a language not of our making, sounds and syllables that signal away from our meanings to a new place, not of our making. I quote Gadamer (1993) here:

> We say that we 'conduct' a conversation, but the more genuine a conversation is, the less its conduct lies within the will of either partner. Thus a genuine conversation is never the one that we wanted to conduct. Rather, it is more generally more correct to say that we fall into conversation, or even that we become involved in it. (p. 383)

Gadamer (1993) writes that "Among the greatest insights that Plato's account of Socrates affords us is that, contrary to the general opinion, it is more difficult to ask questions than to answer them" (p. 362). We must recognize and claim our ignorance or not-knowing before we can seek to know or to understand. We seek the question, the indeterminate, before attempting the answer. For Gadamer the art of questioning is the art of questioning even further which eventually he terms the art of "thinking."

For Gadamer a "genuine" conversation is one that has a life of its own, a shared communication that goes beyond what any one participant has to include. The participants are led by the conversation itself in that the exchange of language evokes a new, becoming entity beyond the limits of each speaker. In each speaker's openness to the views of other speakers lies the possibility for something new and different (1993, p. 367). That openness is the quality that accompanies the trustworthy, a rare and precious occasion of teaching and learning for students and teachers. The air is electric with meanings, intents, desires, fears, hopes.

A critical educator such as Freire (1987) will make rich pedagogical use of the idea that "Dialogue is a moment where humans meet to reflect on their reality as they make and remake it. ... Through dialogue, reflecting together on what we know and don't know, we can then act critically to transform reality" (Shor and Freire, 1987, pp. 98–99). Freire (1970) speaks of the teacher here:

> The teacher is no longer merely the one-who-teaches, but one who is himself taught in dialogue with the students, who in turn while being taught also teach. They become jointly responsible for a process in which all grow. Here, no one teaches another, nor is anyone self-taught. Men teach each other, mediated by the world, by the cognizable objects. (p. 67)

Gallagher (1992) tells us that for many hermeneuticists, conversation and emancipation are essentially linked to the project of transformation. Conversation, the dialectical process of dialogue, can become the heart of a dialogic form of education. Can there be a place for speaking, for voice, for conversation within the classroom? Is this a reform worthy of encouraging in the classroom?

In an eight-year study of schooling completed in the 1980s, John Goodlad found that teachers spent 75% of classroom time on instruction; nearly 70% of this time was "teacher-talk." A scant 5% of instructional time was designed to stir students' anticipation of needing or wanting to respond to the teachers' instructions. Unfortunately, less than 1% of the time required free response involving student opinion or thought (Goodlad, 1984, p. 229).

Are conversations directly linked to and an integral component of learning situations in many schools? The "spectator theory of knowledge" (Doll, 1993, pp. 139–140, 168–169), so firmly entrenched in our schools, seems to be an innate and unconscious part of many teachers' perception of teaching and learning which effectively voids almost all possibility of conversation. For when only one person speaks in the voice of authority and tradition, no one else can find the space to speak.

If we agree with Gadamer that we should "seek to recover and reclaim the sense in which dialogue is the very quintessence of our being-in-the-world" (Bernstein, 1987, p. 518), then the spaces and possibilities for conversations within the classroom that lead to deeper and richer understanding of not only subject matter but student experiences must be forged from the obdurate landscape of schooling. Somehow we must muster Bernstein's "passionate practical commitment" necessary to realize the belief of educational philosopher John Dewey in "genuine communication, dialogue, or critical encounter based on mutual understanding" (p. 511).

At this point, I have traced the effects of *silencing*, the empowerment of *voice*, and the necessity of *conversation*. In this last section, I describe *experience* that will serve as the basis for *conversation*. For if we speak, we must speak about something to someone. I wish to suggest that the lived experiences of the students themselves are not only worthy of research effort but also crucial to the development and implementation of a pedagogy that allows for full student development and growth as human beings in a living, vital society, the cornerstone of educational reform. The shared lived experiences of the teacher are part and parcel of the whole.

(Re)empowering Experience: Lessons of (In)finitude

Ira Shor (1992) in his work *Empowering education: Critical teaching for social change* points to the need for the development of what he terms a "third idiom" for dialogue in the classroom. Through critical dialogue, teachers and students recreate their relationship as well as their methods of communication. Teachers and students within more traditional and less transactional modes of pedagogy use different modes of discourse. There teachers speak in the authoritative tones of organized knowledge at the center of the educational process while students bring to the classroom concrete language and experience in nonacademic tone and style.

However, the dialogic process brought about by critical pedagogy transforms the students' and teacher's different modes of discourse into a new discourse, "the third idiom, which relates academic language to concrete experience and colloquial discourse to critical thought" (p. 255). Going on to claim that the invented third idiom "philosophizes experience while experientializing philosophy" (p. 255), Shor rightly links education to dialogue to experience to philosophy. Nor is he the first to do so.

John Dewey had a lifelong concern for the inescapable importance of everyday experience for the philosophical method, not to mention its ineluctable relationship with education. Dewey (1981) writes that philosophy has the task of "creating and promoting a respect for concrete human experience and its potentialities"

(p. 249). More tellingly, he exhorts that "no philosopher can get away from experience even if he wants to" (p. 273).

Dewey calls for a study not of philosophy but a study of life-experience. Dewey (1981/1973) proposes:

> We always live at the time we live and not at some other time, and only by extracting at each present time the full meaning of each present experience are we prepared for doing the same thing in the future. This is the only preparation which in the long run amounts to anything. (p. xix)

If experience itself and experience that leads to future experience are, according to Dewey, so crucial to philosophy, indeed, to life itself, we must now attempt to understand how Dewey conceptualizes the notion of experience as well as consider how the "speaker" Gadamer develops his analysis of the word experience. I find the work of both philosophers, John Dewey and Hans-Georg Gadamer, fundamental to this research project that rests on a critical and pragmatic treatment of hermeneutics, as well as considers the axioms of radical hermeneutics. I locate my theorizing in many domains of thought as this theorizing presents itself to my years as a teacher. The echoes of thought, past lessons on soaring black chalkboards, bruised and worn books, blue-lined papers, chewed pencils, bits of poetry, lines of prose all wander through my memory and connect in multiple ways to classrooms that have faded away into curling wisps of dreams.

Dewey develops two major principles of experience: the category of continuity or the experiential continuum and the category of interaction. Always working toward the conceptual and practical undermining of Cartesian dualities, Dewey is concerned with refuting the idea that experience is something strictly subjective, psychical, or going on exclusively in someone's mind. The principle of continuity of experience is based upon the biological (as it relates to actual life) habit whose basic characteristic is that every experience enacted or undergone modifies the person who participates in the experience. This modification itself affects the quality and substance of subsequent experiences. Therefore, the principle of continuity of experience means that each experience not only takes up something from those experiences which are prior to it but also modifies in some manner those which follow (Dewey, 1938, p. 33).

The second principle of interaction conflates both factors in an experience—the objective and the internal factors. One has an experience in an environment, affecting an interaction between the persons and their surroundings (Dewey, 1938, p. 35). We live in the world. This interaction forms what Dewey terms a "situation." We are situated within a particular environment that includes the domains of nature, social structure, religion, ethnic group, economic level, educational discourse, language community. We act as we are acted upon. We modify as we are modified. We speak a language even as it speaks us. The past lives on as we live the present and form the future.

For Dewey living and experiencing are one and the same, equal categories of existence. That the living and experiencing are situated within particular domains and are integral interacting entities locates the individual within a particular environment, acting and being acted upon in an interacting process. We add the notion of the subconscious and the realm of the imaginary and the playfulness of the sign to Dewey's brand of pragmatic realism to strengthen our concept of experience.

Perhaps pertinent to our study and the critical effort to reclaim voice is that Dewey also stresses the active participation of an individual in his life experiences. He portrays the individual as "an agent—a reactor, one trying experiments, one concerned with undergoing in a way which may influence what is still to happen" (1938, p. 63). John E. Smith (1987) writes that Dewey "made paramount the idea of transformation and construed experience in terms of its role in resolving problematic situations or in transforming the indeterminate, unsatisfactory situation into a determinate and non-problematic one" (p. 85). Perhaps it is possible only to transform one problematic situation at a time or perhaps it is possible only to partially transform a problematic situation. Permanent solutions to ever-changing problems are not a possibility. However, to struggle and to transform in the midst of daily life experiences become a focus for one's life.

Just as Gadamer finds that "experience of itself seeks and finds words that express it" (1993, p. 417), Dewey writes in *Experience and Education* (1938) that "all human experience is ultimately social: that it involves contact and communication" (p. 38). Dewey takes the contents of the experience of individuals and finds them to be the result of multiple interactions between people and their environments. Because these interactions take place, not only within the person's solitary mind, but also within a particular embedded location, language, and culture, these interactions become a public happening. These public happenings are something to be shared, must be shared. We speak and act together (Smith, 1987, p. 86).

The struggle, the transformation, the ability to presence oneself in one's world is possible if it is acknowledged that one is an integral part of life itself—acting and reacting in an endless sequence of uncertain events. Like the conversation that modifies those participating and is, in turn, modified by those participating, our lives are lived even as we struggle to live them. We must and can speak even as we are spoken.

Reminding us of Dewey's notion that we can only experience our lives within the world and as an embedded part of the world, Dilthey sees our experiences as "a realm before subject and object, a realm in which the world and our experience of it are given together" (Palmer, 1969, p. 109). While we find in Dewey's principle of continuity of experience the idea that every experience both takes up something from prior happenings and modifies in some way that which comes after, we learn from Dilthey that the "past and future form a structural unity with the presentness of all experience and this temporal context is the inescapable horizon within which any perception in the present is interpreted" (Palmer, 1969, p. 110).

While our historical "horizon" is "inescapable," yet we find it possible to scan our horizon as well as that of others in the search for those places that our particular horizons overlap or border one another. For Gadamer our horizons, our preconceptions, prejudices and tradition are what make us able to understand those of someone else (Outhwaite, 1990, p. 27). In effect we are our prejudices, preconceptions, prior experiences. We bring ourselves to an experience, a conversation, and encounter, perhaps, a situation or individual radically different to us, interact in some fashion and communicate, and through the process of interaction with the "other," the "fusion of horizons," become a new being. Gadamer (1992) writes:

> Where one is not concerned with learning how to control something, we will always and again learn through experiencing our own biases, the other-ness of the other in its other-being. To participate with the other and to be a part of the other is the most and the best that we can strive for and accomplish. (p. 235)

He requests and recommends that we "experience the other ... , as the other of our self, in order to participate with one another" (p. 236).

We find ourselves in the world. Dewey (1981) speaks to my private sorrows when he speaks of experience as the "process of standing something; of suffering and passion ... " (p. 63). What he terms the "duplicity of experience" acknowledges the precariousness of stability, the "trials and tests of ourselves" (p. 63). In the second chapter of *Experience and Nature*, Dewey recognizes that "man finds himself living in an aleatory world; his existence involves, to put it badly, a gamble. The world is a scene of risk; it is uncertain, unstable, uncannily unstable" (p. 278). Dewey's humanness, his willingness to speak to the sorrows, perils, and chance happenings of everyday living, validate my own longings to deal with the pain and alienation of our lives.

In similar fashion, Gadamer says that "Experience is a matter of multisided disillusionment based on expectation; only in this way is experience acquired. The fact that 'experience' is preeminently painful and unpleasant does not really color experience black; it lets us see into the inner nature of experience" (Palmer, 1969, p.196; Gadamer, 1993, p. 356). Thus, through suffering we learn the lessons of existence. We catch transitory glimpses of our finitude. Gadamer (1993) writes:

> Thus experience is experience of human finitude. The truly experienced person is one who has taken this to heart, who knows that he is master neither of time nor the future. The experienced man knows that all foresight is limited and all plans uncertain. In him is realized the truth value of experience. (p. 357)

Even so, the pain and struggles of life are yet part of our stories as they weave and unweave in the telling.

After the sudden loss of two of the research participants in a car accident the year of the original study, we searched for the words to express our individual and shared pain as we worked in collaborative inquiry to interpret data or student text. As it turned out, this search for expressions of the meaning of life and death became part of the final hermeneutic conversation of students' experiences. For Gadamer, the contingencies of life and the hard lesson of finitude teach us that we must acknowledge the limits of all anticipation and the tentativeness of our plans (Palmer, 1969, p. 196). However, rather than becoming paralyzed by our experiences of failed expectations and "best laid schemes," we curiously grow even more open to new possibilities, further experience.

Gadamer (1993) poses experience as a "process" (p. 353). The negativity of our experiences has a productive effect in that it either confirms our expectations or it teaches us to adjust to a different outcome. Rather than clinging rigidly to the notion of certainty, we move in sometimes incalculable directions. We learn to expect the unexpected and deal with the not always planned. Our new experiences are less novel through the lessons of those past. The experienced person "acquires a new openness to new experiences" (Gadamer, 1993, p. 357).

We learn to speak to each other of our lives and all that they encompass, our similarities and our differences. We share our experiences and, in the sharing, understand each other more fully, draw a little closer to each other and a little further from the outer limits that separate us. Because of our past experiences, we become "well equipped to have new experiences and to learn from them" (Gadamer, 1993, p. 355). After all, as "the pragmatists tell us, what matters is our loyalty to other human beings clinging together against the dark, not our hope of getting things right" (Rorty, 1982, p. 166). We cling, knowing there are no right answers.

chapter **four**

EXPERIENCING THE RESEARCH JOURNEY: MAPPING THE CURRICULAR AND PERSONAL LIFE-WORLD

As a hermeneutic analysis, the existential analytic succeeds only if it brings to words what we have all along understood about ourselves but have thus far been more or less unable to say.

—J.D.Caputo, 1987, p. 81

The curriculum tends to function in the South not unlike a secular version of biblical fundamentalism, in which the letter of text is mistaken for its spirit.

—William F. Pinar, 2004, p. 240

The purpose of all interpretation is to conquer a remoteness, a distance between the past cultural epoch to which the text belongs and the interpreter himself. By overcoming this distance, by making himself contemporary with the text, the exegete can appropriate its meaning to himself: foreign, he makes it familiar, that is, he makes it his own. It is thus the growth of his own understanding of the other. Every hermeneutics is thus, explicitly or implicitly, self-understanding by means of understanding others.

—Paul Ricoeur, 1974, pp. 16–17

With tickets in hand and travel brochures as guides, she begins the trip with uncertainty as to final destination or definite purpose of perambulations. The journey itself unfolds along the way as events present themselves and locations appear. The final importance of the journey or the events that occur along the way are relived at journey's end through the telling, the recreating of the narrative forms of life. The adventure of life, the journey, is a metaphor for all, whether one lives the hero's life of Odysseus or the miserable existence of Edith Wharton's Lily Bart (1905/1984).

As I lay claim to the autobiographical and methodological attempt to understand my own life journey as a teacher and the educational journeys of my students, I think of the past, my own historicity, that in forming and informing the present will, in turn, shape the future. I realize that such an understanding cannot be separated from the past that encompasses the realms of tradition and culture. Just as Odysseus felt a compelling need in the house of Alcinous, King of Phaeacia, to retell the story of his ten-year wanderings, I retell parts of my past and the past of this high school in the attempt to understand how past experiences inform the present. Have I come home to safety? Can I? I have moved in never-ending circles of time, place, events, and language that have formed my life even as I partially (in)formed myself. As interpreter of my students' writings and tales of their educational pasts, I turn my attention to the "hermeneutical situation" (Gadamer, 1993, pp. 301–302). We travel there.

(Re)telling My Past: Locating the Present

Smoothened Arkansas mountain ranges slope southward to the north Louisiana red clay that sucks fast the shallow roots of the swaying, pole-like pine trees. The verdant pines bend obligingly to the wind's whims and kindly lend their sharp-needled spikes to mark rusty-colored pathways. The trees stand as pungent sentries to two-tracked, narrow wagon roads that, at the end of the nineteenth century, led from one farming community to the next—Pine Grove, Macedonia, Mars Hill, Walker Creek, Antioch, Sike's Ferry, Shongaloo.

The farming community, dubbed Barefoot Station and bounded by virgin stands of timber and home to squatter's shacks, plunged into nineteenth century progress when the Piney Woods Lumber Company began sawmill operations in 1894. Natural springs flowing from sloping hills proved themselves elemental to the community's existence and Barefoot Station renamed itself Spring.

"The Company" or the Bodcaw (Bodcau) Lumber Company of Stamps, Arkansas, "owned Spring—the houses, the land, the only store, and later the post office" (*The Spring Press & News Journal*, 14 Mar, 1979). In 1902, the lumber company furnished sawn boards and manpower to construct a two-story white frame building that served as school, church, and community house on the Plain Dealing highway. Later, in 1909, four high school classrooms were provided in a two-story structure added perpendicularly to the original building. Spring High School graduated its first class in 1911: 16 boys and 8 girls (all white). In a group photograph, I peer at the girls in long, billowing skirts and puffed sleeved blouses sitting primly with hands folded in their laps while the boys stand with arms folded or hands on hips, jacketed with bowler hats on their heads. All look straight ahead into the future.

In 1937, a paper company had begun operations south of the main sections of the town. By the time of my graduation from high school, my father and thousands of other men and women had been employed in the sprawling factory for nearly thirty years. Everyone's father seemed to either work at the "mill" or operate a small business on the single street that stretched for five or six blocks—Main Street. The "company," the town, the school, the church—all were still as intertangled as they had been in the beginnings of the farming and timber community.

Fifty-three years after that first graduation in 1911, in May of 1964, I graduated from Spring High School with a class of 127 students (still all white) in the cavernous auditorium of the red-orange brick building constructed on the former location of the earlier town's white section, nicknamed strangely enough "Egypt." Lauded as "64 Senior Class One of the Best" (*The Axe*, 21 May, 1964), one-third of my class maintained a "B" or better scholastic average throughout the four years of high school. According to the yearly attendance records of the *Green Leaf Register*, the promotion rates for grades 9 through 12 were 96.1%, 97.4%, 94.1%, and 98%, respectively. However, the highest enrollment figure of 162 was for the school year 1961–62. Graduating 127 and losing a total of 35 students through moving, dropping out due to grades, or being overage, my class (1964) actually graduated 78% of the highest original enrollment figure. I just do my numbers slant, having been poetized by Emily Dickinson to "Tell all the Truth but tell it slant."

My years are gone, except for residual memories, faint and far-off, and tell-tell marks of experience though the buildings stand static and staid. The Spring High School graduating class of 1992–93 included 83 students. The year of this class's highest original enrollment was 1990–91 with a total of 132 students. Graduation rate based on the highest total original enrollment figure of 1990–91 (132) was 62%. The *Green Leaf Register* boasts yearly promotion rates for grades 9 through twelve of 81.15%, 78%, 82%, and 98%, respectively. The discrepancy between yearly promotion rates and a graduation rate based upon the year of highest enrollment is submerged in multilayers of yellowed pages of *Green Leaf Registers* stacked on dusty shelves in the school safe. I found them.

More positive reports are recorded and filed. According to the Louisiana Committee which compiled the annual report of instructional personnel "Commission on Secondary Schools, Southern Association of Colleges and Schools," Spring High School is a public high school first accredited in 1954. The school includes grades 9–12 with a total enrollment of 490 students and 29 on staff (25 classroom teachers, 1 principal, 1 assistant principal, 1 librarian, and 1 guidance counselor).

As might be expected from the close community and school ties to the timber and lumber industries, the school mascot is a muscled lumberjack. "Axe 'em, Jacks" is the frequently heard cheer at all sports activities. The football team weekly surges through huge, hooped circles of white paper with a black and gold-colored figure of a massive lumberjack, axe in hand, held in place before each game by smiling cheerleaders as they balance on each other's shoulders. I used to be one of those smiling girls, ponytail spinning and heart racing in short pleated skirt with matching sweater, a huge "S" sewn on the front. In typical Southern fashion, Spring is known throughout the area as a football town. Where else can we excel? How can parents feel the thrill of victory or the down of defeat?

This school year, the year of our study, the head football coach of some thirty years tragically suffered a heart attack during a home football game on the side lines and was rushed to a hospital where he later died. The somber football team, dressed in black and gold jerseys, sat in the choir loft during the funeral service at a small Missionary Baptist church, the coach's home church. Metal folding chairs set up in the church yard accommodated the overflowing crowd. The loss was dutifully and thoroughly covered on the evening news of the three Shreveport television stations as well as recorded in *The Times* and *The Spring Press & News Journal*.

Indeed sports are a prime focus of our school staff. Eight of the 25 classroom teachers either teach exclusively physical education classes or split their teaching duties between the classroom and the football field, basketball court, baseball field, or golf course. In addition to these eight coaches, both our principal and assistant principal spend a portion of their time in coaching duties. Our assistant principal was named temporary head football coach after the death of the head coach.

The incoming freshman class of 1992–93 had an original total enrollment of 140: 86 white students (53 boys, 33 girls) and 54 African American students (24 boys, 30 girls). The numerical gap in this ninth grade class between white and African American boys is quite large while the number of African American and white girls is roughly equivalent. The figures are evident in the racial and gender makeup of my research group: 7 white boys, 2 white girls, and 1 African American girl. The research group is composed of those students who were enrolled in both my accelerated English I and Spanish I classes. There were no black boys in either of these classes, of course, but that is another issue. In hindsight, obviously, I should have included an African American male student or two for balance. How to balance what is askew?

However, the members of my research group were drawn from my English I and Spanish I classes. The research participants also chose to work with this project after an initial meeting to introduce and discuss the purpose and focus of the study. The hook for the group seemed to be the appeal to make the spaces available for conversation about students' experiences of schooling. Though I worked with all of the students in three English classes and two Spanish classes throughout the entire school year, I worked most intensively with these students during the latter part of the second semester. The conversation began. We spoke. Sometimes hesitatingly, sometimes loudly, sometimes not at all.

Stalking Meaning: Questioning Curriculum

As Gadamer (1960/1993, p. 299) finds that "The essence of the question is to open up possibilities and keep them open," I allowed the realization of my lack of understanding of how my students experienced schooling and their lives within my classroom and with others to outline broad parameters of inquiry. The basic phenomenological questions that we attempted to work with were as simple as life is complicated:

- How do students experience curriculum?
- How are they able to understand these experiences?
- How do they express these understandings?

In describing and discussing these remembered and lived experiences as much as possible in experiential terms, we focused on particular situations or events.

Van Manen (1990) stresses that the purpose of phenomenological research is to learn from other people's experiences and their reflections on these experiences in order to come to a deeper and better understanding of the significance of a particular aspect of human life within the context of the whole of human experience (p. 54). The deeper goal of phenomenological research is to continue asking the question of what is the nature of the phenomenon as an "essentially human experience."

The starting point of our project was what van Manen (1990) terms the "empirical realm of everyday lived experience" (p. ix). The research participants began by writing about current subjects being taken, ranking classes in order of importance, thinking about possible learning needs and interests, and continued through the study with a consideration of relationships with individual teachers and comprehension of self and others.

The writings and conversations moved through layers of time and experiences and shifted back and forth between the individual student and others. Through dialogue journaling, group and class discussions, writings in response to literature that dealt with students and school, and free response writings that searched for individual experiences and memories, we attempted to allow ourselves "to see," to reflect upon these experiences in order to develop a new consciousness of ourselves and our experiences.

Like Sartre, "We would be stalkers of meaning" (Merleau-Ponty, 1964, p. ix). In so doing, we enabled ourselves to make some type of sense of our experiences from the center, from within, and notice how these meanings interacted with those forces of our lives that were found without, either our felt consciousnesses or immediate environments. The interpretation of these experiences was and continued, throughout the writing of this project, to be an interactive process. According to Gallagher (1992), the task of hermeneutics is to locate and specify different factors, including the epistemological, sociological, cultural, and linguistic factors that affect the interpretative process. The ongoing recursive process of interpretation was embedded within the project of dialogic communication (Gallagher, 1992, pp. 75–76).

Language was a focus as it interacted with our school setting and played a part in our abilities to interpret our lifeworlds. Perhaps it is only the catalyst of understanding. Perhaps it places limits and marks the parameters of understanding. While recognizing the limitations that language placed upon our understanding, we also realized that language enables partial access to textual and lived meanings, at least a beginning of possibility. Perhaps we might consider Derrida's notion that "true language is not language at its most human but language at its most language-y, language at its most self-sufficient, even to the extent of being independent of human beings" (Harland, 1987, p. 125). Language escapes our best attempts at understanding; language moves sideways when human intent is to move forward; language wavers and wobbles when we thrust it firmly against thought. Is this the "aporia of conversation" that is "caught between trust and suspicion" (Gallagher, 1992, p. 23)? Is our use of language caught between intent of the speaker and interpretation of the listener? It falters. In early translations of this study, I called upon Ricoeur's "hermeneutics of trust" (Gallagher, 1992, p. 21) that allows for the possibility of shared meanings, conversation, and transformation. In later work done as a group, we searched ourselves for variance, subtle shades of meaning as we reinterpreted our language. However, as stated earlier, the later attempt did not succeed. That may be another study.

Through dialogical conversation, the means by which meanings are shared and created in reciprocity, and the evolution of the "texts" that shape our lives, we sought a "fusion of horizons" (Gadamer, 1993, pp. 302–307), common grounds of some sort for developing new understandings. The first task was to determine our own horizons—mine and those of the research participants. We began with a situated school setting and attempted to "re-see" our own embedded positions. Gadamer (1993) defines *horizon* as "the range of vision that includes everything that can be seen from a particular vantage point" (p. 302). We attempted to see our lives from within the middle of our school experiences.

One must be aware of one's own horizon as well as be able to see beyond it. Rather than existing as a static entity, the horizon moves with one, changing as one changes, broadening as one broadens thought or knowledge. We form our present by living in ways formed by our past. Just as the horizon of the present is to be understood in terms of the past, we understand each other by mapping those places in which we form lives that are blends of not only past experiences but connections to the experiences shared with one another.

As I attempted to make possible the space for a "fusion of horizons" that takes place in and through understanding our own situatedness, I came more and more to realize that this event is "actually the achievement of language" (Gadamer, 1993, p. 378). The conversations that take place between teacher and students, between students and students move through language toward a common, if contested, ground of understanding and experience. That which was becomes something new, a curious blend of present and future. What the teacher thought or proposed becomes transformed in the process of open communication with students. In turn, the students' thoughts or proposals are also transformed in the transaction of dialogue. Gadamer (1993) writes: "To reach an understanding in a dialogue is not merely a matter of putting oneself forward and successfully asserting one's own point of view, but being transformed into a communion in which we do not remain what we were" (p. 379). We sought connections and change and transformation. That these connections are tentative and tenuous, of course, is acknowledged. That I, in my writing, make my own meanings is hard to refute. We accept the (dis)connections and (un)change and (re)formation that is located in the spaces-between and locations-submerged.

Situated Horizon: Past and Present Narratives

I begin with my own horizon. I attempt to write the personal narrative with awareness that memory is faulty, deceptive, sometimes self-serving, often painful. Grumet (1990) informs my perspective as she considers the use of language, acknowledging the deconstructive difficulties of indeterminancy, historical contingencies, social constructions. Still she informs that writing is "inner and outer, personal and public, spontaneous and considered, mind and body" (p. 321). Grumet discusses autobiography as "relating (it) to some conversation real or imagined which I have had with someone else, and at the same time the text which I produce is dear to me like my own body" (p. 321). We are always speaking to ourselves as well as to others, writing and rewriting until we exhaust the details or unconsciously suppress the unwanted memories. Revising endlessly we write our existence.

And so I remember the ninth grade and 1960 at Spring High School in the small town that was my world. The sixties and high school came in juxtaposition that fall. An era had ended; a new one had begun. Uninvited, unwanted, necessary, transforming changes intruded. Moving across the four-lane highway 7 from the familiar, familial junior high school to the sprawling terrain of the high school seemed like a perilous leap to the adult world. The class schedule was complicated and confusing (first bell, tardy bell, 4A lunch, 4B lunch, homeroom, club day schedule); the low-slung buildings loomed overwhelmingly with narrow halls going in myriad directions.

The upperclassmen stood heads higher than we—clad in starched blouses with Peter Pan collars and circle pins. They seemed in possession of prior knowledge denied fledgling freshmen. Senior football players monitored the halls during lunch hours while the faculty smoked away the break in separate lounges for men and women teachers. We were uneasy, unsettled. The hackles were up; the scent of change was in the air. The crime rate would double this decade; local, state, and federal expenditures for police doubled; the inventor of the term "rock and roll" would be indicted for accepting payola; groups of courageous African American students would refuse to stand while not being served at a lunch counter in Woolworth's in Charlotte, North Carolina. The sixties blew in with a gusty purpose and will.

I was hardly aware of the larger society. My world was small and narrow. I moved between a 50s vintage red brick box of a house with a tidily planted garden of beds of spring pansies and Saint Augustine grass and the elongated high school bound by asphalt streets and cracked sidewalks. In between lay a Baptist church, that bastion of morality and authority. At a far distance of some five miles was International Paper Company where my father worked different shifts as an electrician.

There was a social and economic gulf among paper mill worker, paper mill supervisor, and business owner, not to mention a racial gulf as wide as an ocean. Somehow my mother managed to straddle the narrow gulf, not the wider one, by playing inspired bridge, spearheading the annual March of Dimes effort, and joining the Civic Club. An intelligent, verbal, and tense woman, an avid reader who had graduated from high school as valedictorian in 1936, she spoke the social discourse of those with "more." Her daughter must learn the same language, a bastardized approach to civil behavior.

I took dance lessons with the "privileged" at twelve, learning to foxtrot and waltz, in preparation for country club dances for younger teenagers. The sting of rejection lingers as I remember the remark made by a classmate at school the year of the dance lessons—"It's just like inviting yourself to a birthday party." I assume that my mother called the couple giving dance lessons, asking permission for my participation in the classes. I grimly went and moved in either stiff circles or wavering squares with awkward boys. My mother hosted a birthday party for me in our home for these same children. They came. We danced. I did not belong. I sensed, felt, not understood, the differences between myself and the others.

Church membership was a comforting if boring fact of life. Comforting and boring were bordered by an aesthetic experience as well, one of the first I remember. The wine purple cushions and the Gothic stained glass window seemed beautiful enough for God, at least to me. I felt He was honored. Surely we were all bound in equality for the glory of heaven, an eternity of sunny, somniferous Sundays. The church rose like a giant mammoth of gray blocks of stone on Arkansas Street, sprung straight from the red clay. Guardian of public and private morality, the semi-gothic structure with Mondrian-like stained glassed panels of red, green, yellow, blue (multicolored like Joseph's coat), of arched windows and massive oak, carved doors was as beautiful to me as anything I could imagine. Inside was a cavelike hush—dark and holy. The pews were layered and padded with wine-colored velvet, buttoned and tufted cushions. I sat each Sunday and counted not my sins but the tiles in the cathedral ceiling, as high above my head and being as heaven.

I sat each day in my classes: English, civics, Algebra I, general science, typing, and physical education. I counted not my learning but the lines on the paper. In silence I absorbed enough to make the required grades. Yet, my real learning lay in my own reading: Dickens, Charlotte Bronte, Richard Halliburton, Ogden Nash, Steinbeck, Cervantes. If my teachers had real blood that surged through corporeal flesh, I was not aware. I was muffled, surrounded by a stillness that I camouflaged that year by dressing in the pep squad uniform, gold sweater and black swinging skirt, and screaming wildly for the football team. The public sphere of a pep rally in the auditorium or a bonfire at the stadium was in counterpoint to the private isolation of the classroom, indeed of my entire life.

I bring this consciousness of my own ninth grade to a consideration of this research group of ninth graders. Their world is different than mine. Their world proceeds from mine. I smile at them as they come in the room; I hope they feel more connected to what we are learning, that they feel more alive, less isolated than I did. I wonder if I teach to relive my past, to create a better, more viable version of my own school years. Am I making up for the past? Are we always recreating our lives? Reinventing ourselves?

Situated Discourse: Processing Schooling and Students

The research group of ten students attended my second hour English I class and fifth hour Spanish I class. Since the fifth hour was preceded by a recess, we might steal extra time to work together. I made a list and asked the students if they would agree to participate voluntarily. They seemed intrigued by it all; the curiosity and interest I saw in their eyes during class spilled over into this project. Once they understood that I was after an understanding of their understanding, a seeming redundancy of words, they eagerly wrote on and discussed our topics. I locate myself again, this time submerged in a deluge of data.

Each student brought his or her personality and experiences to our shared conversations. In retrospect I think I found some part of myself in each one. I was a freshman again. I found the serious, the silly, the vain, the profound, the talker, the listener, the thinker, the doer. I tell myself that this must be why I feel so connected to this group, so much a part of their lives. At the same time, I realize that I am not. We studied English, Spanish, and ourselves that ninth grade year.

Time passed. They began the tenth grade as we met to discuss my initial interpretations. One had moved. Two had died. They no longer were—my group, my students, my work, my connections to learning. We are no longer what we were. I focus on each one and attempt to create portraits of these students that picture their school lives and introduce them as research participants. Again, time, that old man, has passed. They are now adults. Part of the group meets again to reinterpret our lives. They are still my students. In disguise. We peer through the past, seeking present connections. Perhaps they are not there, not possible.

Crossing the Line: The Life of the Student

Emma, a pert and delicate girl with long wisps of hair that curve around her cheeks, keeps a faithful record of her school life in her journal by chronicling her feelings and experiences with poetry and pictures. I write in my journal (22 March 1993): She keeps a journal that bares her soul, normal topics, love, boys, friendship, all of the standard stuff that she makes important because of her sincere desire to deal with the issues in her life. She worries the notion that others think her an "airhead" when she probably thinks more deeply and feels more acutely than many. I learn from her how strongly a teenage girl can feel about friendships, relationships, and her own life. Today Emma is a counselor at a facility for troubled youth. In conversation it is evident that she relates. She still seeks and outlines the intricacies of relationships between herself and others.

Alicia carries the heavy weight of the world on her solid shoulders. A mature girl, she comes to school with her family and religious background as strong presences in her behavior and speech. Quiet and sedate, her concern and care for others—students and teachers—lead her through the school day. The teenage rebellion is foreign to her mind as she makes herself a part of the student and adult worlds, somehow at the same time. She is a peacemaker. She anchored and supported me and our project. Now Alicia has become a secondary teacher in her own right, teaching social studies and journalism. Her common sense approach to life steadies her pedagogical practice with adolescents.

Veronica, an African American student, is the epitome of a child-already-adult with serious glasses and no-nonsense, severely pulled back ponytail. Self-possessed and assured of where she is going in life, straight toward success, she placed first in Spanish I at District Literary Rally. Veronica was also quiet in the classroom and worked at a self-determined speed. Her goal was, I think, to be always first. At the same time, she and Alicia laughed and talked with their classmates as some of the boys cut up and cause small disturbances (petite disarrays). Her smile came slowly and worked its way up to her brown eyes. One would call her in an emergency for help or ask if one's slip were showing. She would smile slowly and tell you, amused at your helplessness. Veronica still smiles in amusement at the comments of others in our discussion groups. She is now raising two small daughters and working as an investigator for various business institutions.

The few-in-number girls were sometimes overshadowed by the more verbal and assertive boys. Although I attempted to clear paths for their voices in group discussions, the unusual group of lively boys quite often overpowered them. Two of the quieter, though not less thoughtful, were John and Mark. John was a tall, lanky boy who would blend into the green walls, chameleon-like, if allowed. Reluctant to speak out, he saw the offside of things and was not lacking in critical perspective. After writing this section and transcribing recorded group discussions, I must add that while John was quiet in class, during our lengthy group conversations, he quite often held forth quite strongly on classroom issues as he also did in later sessions of interpretative inquiry. I find that I am curious why he was so silent during class and then became quite vocal in the small group. His participation in our later work was thoughtful and critical.

Mark was his counterpoint, quiet as well, thinking also, but along more conventional lines. He had little to say during classes or the group discussions. Serious about his learning and work, as was his older brother while in my classes, Mark's even disposition and mild-mannered participation offered a calming balance to the zaniness of some of the other members. With brownish hair, spectacled dark eyes, and slight frame, he was willing to act as foil to and appreciator of the sometimes "wild" times in the classroom. He smiled quietly as his eyes filled with the pleasure, the amore, of the enacted dramas. He moved the year following the initial research project.

The fair-haired Chris also was quiet and thinking, but ready to join in any highjinks initiated by some of the others if not surreptitiously orchestrated by him from across the width of the classroom. I tiptoed around his moods. One of my colleagues has since said: "Chris knew the dark angels" (conversation, 17 Nov 93). One late winter morning during English class while the others were reading, he and I watched out the dusty windows shrouded by bedraggled blinds as a flock of ravenous robins ate the red berries of a towering holly tree across the street.

Later that year, while in Spanish I class, Chris threw a pencil on the floor and, with a smirky smile, dared all—"Cross that line!" I did, I tried to cross the line to the deeper recesses of his mind where he kept secure his darker thoughts. The stony dissatisfaction on his face forced me to face the fact that many students go through the day with only a sense of ennui as companion. Only occasionally could either he or I hold it at bay. We tried. The next year, the second year of the project, the same green tower had replenished its bounty of berries; I stared at the rounded redness during sessions of interpretation with Chris's classmates Jimmy and Carl. At the same time, we talked about Chris and what his loss meant to us.

Ryan was another student who kept things bottled somewhere deep inside himself. A master of detailed, descriptive writing, he perhaps was the most self-isolated of the group, though well-liked by all. Repressed in someway somehow by his life or by a school life that demanded such rigid conformity, he seemed uneasy as he made his way. I find my own writing stymied by the feelings of repression that I intuit from his writings and classroom behavior. He wrote in his journal how distant he felt from his teachers. Yet, Ryan is among the more expressive now as if in adulthood he has learned or acquired discursive ability to tease out the meanings of his thoughts. He has worked for philanthropic organizations while studying for a degree in international studies.

Jimmy was the bridge between the quiet and sometimes explosive to the loud and always explosive. The male counterpoint to the maturity of the girls, he carried the genes of my senior high school English teacher that spoke cogently in his writing and thoughts. The grandson of a superb English teacher, he spoke well of his background—religious and familial. He too had feet in both camps—that of the adult and child's world. He too was a peacemaker. My present help in time of need. He continued to be the caregiver, the steady presence of concern, in the stark face of death. Recently his task was to gather the group again, once in the late summer (2003) and again in the fall (2004) of the following year. He led us toward our work of understanding.

Carl brought the role of buffoon into the classroom and our presence. He clowned and talked his way bullishly into our attention. Getting him to write seriously about anything all year was a challenge as he could take any topic and make some seemingly nonsensical something of it. The irony of the nonsense was that, with effort, an actual meaning could be found that he had carefully obscured. He loved to make arguments about just what was and wasn't right about what he had done. His mind shot into tangents from left field to way out of the ballpark. I too laughed with him. Life is a game to be played and enjoyed. His astuteness in the form of a demand for sincerity has continued as an adult who thoughtfully contemplates his future as well as his past while he now plans to become a classroom teacher.

The last boy, my "imaginary student" who played "imaginary games of golf" in the classroom, could soar with angels and commiserate with devils. The bane of many teachers' teaching days, he was, however, a literature student of the best kind—playful, thoughtful, insightful, inspired, and creative. Steinbeck, H.G. Wells, Emily Dickinson, Twain, Dickens were all part of his reading repertoire. Never one to be bored, he not only created on paper but also in the classroom as he orchestrated elaborate distractions. Will was a distractor/actor of the first order, one who could accurately estimate the value of classroom work and react accordingly. He wrote tellingly of the danger of not savoring life's fullest flavor, of the boy "who didn't tell what he feels; he soon lost himself and lost what was real" (class journal, 6 October 1992). To lose his brightness diminished the glow of life in the daily lives of his friends, family, and teachers. A "golden lad." In our recent work we struggled to hear his voice on the tapes of group discussions made during our original study. A faint echo of life. A loss of presence. Loss is one of those spiraling entities, one of those mathematical entities of endless enumeration.

I struggled, along with my research participants, toward finding the right questions to ask, toward securing my attitude in a listening position, and toward attempting to uncover and understand this thing called school. Each of the participants was an invaluable part of the whole—each had a different voice and perspective as well as a different notion of surviving in the school setting. Our task was to separate and sift the strands into a pattern that rendered visible at least a partial glimpse of a whole. In the next chapter I finally attempt to take some of their writings and conversations and explicate possible meanings after chapters of discussion of rationale and methodology. Obviously the process has been as important as, or even more important than, any possibly flawed findings. Isn't the journey as significant as the destination? Perhaps the journey is all that matters. Perhaps the process of learning, the research, the methodologies, the data collection, the reflection, the tentative findings, the parts are greater that their sum. Perhaps this is why I so slowly and carefully work toward the end of this work.

Yet, the clouds darken and move across the sky of perception, only at times does the light of the full moon or the twinkling of the stars make possible a sudden and sharp recognition of the educational landscape, like waiting for one's eyes to become accustomed to the light of a moon- and star-filled sky. I peer into the writings of the participants to look for patterns of meaning to make some sort of sense of our work together. Their journal writings and taped discussions clutter my mind as surely as they fill my dining room table with their scrawling hand scripts across pages and pages of paper and fill my ears with the sounds of their scratchy voices recorded on a cheap tape recorder.

chapter **five**

LIVING THE JOURNEY: SPEAKING THE EXPERIENCES

You may know life by heart, how to walk, talk and breathe. But what is the point of all this if you don't live it?

—JOHN, RESEARCH JOURNAL, 1993

For hermeneutics always has to do with keeping the difficulty of life alive and with keepings its distance from the easy assurances of metaphysics and the consolations of philosophy.

—J. D. CAPUTO, 1987

School experience is more often portrayed in autobiographies as a source of self-alienation which has to be countered and overcome in order to find an authentic voice. Adults who look back to rewrite their school stories attempt implicitly (but more often explicitly) to contest the school's power of characterization and reclaim the authority to create their own identities.

—SUSAN DOUGLAS FRANZOSA, 1992

Written on the last day that the research participants and I recorded thoughts on topics pertaining to curriculum, teachers, self, and others, John's journal entry, quoted above, suddenly led me toward a sharper awareness of what it was that we were searching for in the attempt to understand our school lives—what it means to live a life. Grumet (1992) tells us that:

> The researcher who scrutinizes one person's account of experience must confront the very issues that were debated by Husserl and his existential progeny. To what degree does reflection … distort experience to fit idealized forms? Does the distancing required by the phenomenological perspective break the bonds of commitment and action that tie us to the real world? Who is the self that we attend? Is the reflecting self continuous with the

> acting self? Do our multiple social roles splinter the self into situational poses strung along a temporal chain? (p. 40)

She answers these questions by contrasting autobiographical methods with those of the empiricist who faces similar "quandaries." The difference lies within the context in which autobiographical methods are located. Calling on Freire's thought that "every aspect of a person's interaction with culture, language, and others is saturated with the political reality of his or her situation" (p. 40), Grumet claims that autobiographical methods are "also cognizant of the impact of milieu and address the political present and the subjective past simultaneously" (p. 40). She simply and complexly asks us to acknowledge the "paradox" of our knowings, the illusive nature of the conjoining of the objective and the subjective, the mysteries of knowing and being and living and acting in the world. Again, what does it mean to live a life? What does it mean to suffer the deaths of friends and students? What does it mean to be a student in a school setting? What does it mean to learn? What can we know?

What does it mean to be a student in a school setting? While much research has been done to study the multiple external influences on students with the resultant effects on their learning, Pinar's analysis of, what he terms, "the ways schools make children mad" (Pinar, Reynolds, Slattery, & Taubman, 2002, p. 518) focuses on the internal structures of schooling and strengthens the existential call for an educational reform that negates the deleterious effects of traditional schooling. His list is lengthy but worthy of noting here:

1. hypertrophy or atrophy of fantasy life;
2. division or loss of self to others via modeling;
3. dependence and arrested development of autonomy;
4. criticism by others and the loss of self-love;
5. thwarting of affiliative needs;
6. estrangement from self and its effect upon the process of individuation;
7. self-direction becomes other-direction;
8. loss of self and internalization of externalized self;
9. internalization of the oppressor: development of a false self-system;
10. alienation from personal reality due to impersonality of schooling groups;
11. desiccation via disconfirmation; and
12. atrophy of capacity to perceive esthetically and sensuously.

Indeed, such a lengthy list of dismal and damaging effects of traditional attempts to educate the "young" in this country makes one hang one's chin to chest. Alarming and shaming as the results are of most educational practices, they stand little or no chance of being modified or "reformed" at this time. I feel a little mad myself.

At crisis now in the throes of the federal mandates of No Child Left Behind, educational structures are currently bowing lower to external forces than when Pinar began his study of schooling and the effects of an official and regulated denial of self within the individual. So what are we doing to students in the name of education? This chapter is a partial and incomplete discussion of some of the implications of discussions and writing done by the research group and myself, a faltering and hesitant attempt to make some sort of meaning of our work together. The work on the dining room table has been somewhat coded, organized, and explicated. Most of the tag ends have been neatly folded back. The tendency to make order of chaos has encouraged me to look for more commonalities than (un)commonalities, conclusions that circle back to Aristotle's completeness of plot. Our tragedy does have the necessary elements of Peripety and Discovery as well as that necessary and critical element of Suffering. Our tragedy moves to an end. Of course I am mixing two strands of thought: the tragic results of current educational practices with the loss of two students in the study and the effects of that on the research group.

Learning and Living: Curriculum Conversations

My preliminary findings of the original study included the notion that students were well aware of how teachers teach and how well these same teachers are able to deliver and explain subject content. That they cared so passionately was surprising, in the face of the student apathy so often cited in academic research. Another issue of importance was the idea that teachers needed to bring real life into the classroom, including their own. These students yearned to draw close, in apparent contradiction to the alienation most often attributed to teenagers. They desired to learn subject content, learn the lives of their teachers as connected to this content, and also to learn "self." We turn to the personal as we consider that the loss of the research participants (Chris and Will) in a car accident makes John's observation *that it is of no use to know how to walk, talk, and breathe, if you don't know how to live* even more pertinent and poignant. This exploration of an understanding of the depths of the meanings of life is the whole.

As students, many of us learned discrete bits of information "by heart": the multiplication tables, spelling rules, lists of presidents, the periodic table, verb conjugations, pronoun cases. John warns that even though we move through our days functioning as human beings, living the discrete particulars, we are missing the more crucial aspect of our lives: the sense of what it is that makes us alive as well as the importance of actually "living" the whole of life. All, perhaps, should move beyond simply knowing "life by heart" toward a fuller realization and understanding of the complexities of life as well as becoming more conscious of the everyday particularities of walking, talking, and breathing. Know how to live. That is a significant and difficult suggestion.

Jardine (1992) claims that "hermeneutic inquiry is concerned with the ambiguous nature of life itself" (p. 119). In postpositivist research, the search for a heteroglot of voices, the contradictions of subjectivities, and the essence of the lived moment is an attempt to offer a fleeting glimpse of what it is to be alive—to speak, to listen, to do, to learn, to exist. Not from a desire to present lived ambiguities as "presentable," but from the desire to give "voice" to them, this research project calls forth, evokes, and speaks the metaphors, images, and dreams of our lives. Through a thoughtful discussion of the concrete particulars of the schoolday that detail subject matter, relationships with teachers and how they teach, and relationships with self and others, we search for the voices that more fully and faithfully presence ourselves in the world.

These students, introduced in the preceding chapter, and I wrote in dialogue journals in response to various topics pertaining to school and curriculum for a total of 18 entries over a period of four weeks in the spring of 1993. The dialogue journals, in which the oral process of conversation is mimicked in writing, set the stage for a dialogical inquiry in which the topics evolved as conversational partners interacted through spoken language. Beginning with a heuristic topic that called for the definitions of subject matter, I responded to the participants' writings, which were presentations of very personal reactions to subject matter, by turning to topics that were more oriented to the participants' interests or feelings. In other words, response called for response in reciprocal fashion; writings were based upon writings. I overlay and layered subsequent topics in this manner throughout the collection of participant text as well as throughout the collaborative interpretation of text.

At times, the topic evolved from group discussions. For example, when the participants persisted in calling the group's attention to a stressful situation in a particular class, they introduced the examination of relationships with teachers. In this manner, the participants themselves guided the questioning.

At other times, the topic came from my reading of scholarly texts (Shor, 1992; Gadamer, 1993; van Manen, 1990, 1991). In a sense, I fieldtested philosophical and pedagogical ideas within the classroom. Finally, in an attempt to gain some distance of perspective from self and others, as well as from the confines of the schoolworld, we attempted to create metaphorical representations. In an attempt to remain faithful to the notion of open-ended dialogue (Noddings, 1992, p. 23), the last entry was an invitation to review previous writings and respond with whatever came to the participants' minds.

Though I actually gathered journal writings throughout the schoolyear from three English classes, the interpretation of text (see Rivkin, 1991, p. 68) in this chapter deals with the 180 entries that were written in a concentrated effort at focusing the thoughts of a particular group of students on the topic of school. At the same time that an effort was made to narrow the focus on the particularities of school experiences and to "defamiliarize" the everyday events of school life, a widening of the spectrum of the totality of life experiences came into view as we wrote, discussed, and, later, worked in collaborative inquiry to interpret text.

In addition to these daily writings in the research journals, the participants and I met weekly in fifty-minute group discussions. Gathering for discussions a total of four times during a four-week timeframe, we met for two whole-group discussions the first and last meetings, while meeting in groups of three or four students the second and third meetings. I mixed the makeup of the small group discussions to allow for various patterns of student interaction. We met on Fridays across the hall from our English and Spanish classroom in an abandoned, vandalized room. The scarred desks were raw and peeling, the institutional green walls and chalkboards smeared with benign graffiti. We circled our desks around the tape recorder and began, amidst the dust and disorder of daily school life.

Writing preceded the spoken word. Perhaps I had this in disarray and (dis)arrangement. It is "That Dangerous Supplement ..." (Derrida, 1997/1976, p. 141). While Derrida discusses Rousseau's praise of living speech, he delineates the possibilities of "speech as it should be or rather as it *should have been*" (p. 141). The importance of the verb tense, the perfect conditional, signals an illusive condition, "the mirage of its immediacy," unmitigated by presence and captive to the "speculary dispossession which at the same time institutes and deconstitutes me (is) also a law of language" (p. 141). In continuation of this thought, Derrida sees writing as a strain toward resituating presence and meaning. This "strange unity" of writing and speech is perhaps one of temporary disclosure, partial appearance, and possible difference. We find ourselves in our writing, in our history, in our culture.

As I read and reflected daily upon the writings in the research journals, I reintroduced topics during the weekly discussions for the purposes of expansion and elaboration as well as for varying possibilities of interaction and interpretation among the participants. In this way, the topics were a matter of oral as well as written discourse. Also, during this time, the students brought up for discussion matters that were of concern and importance to them that had been prompted, but not fully addressed, by the writings. I asked the research participants each session to re- read either their journals or a classmate's journal in order to comment or to ask a question concerning some issue raised by the writings. Each session, I waited for the topic to exhaust itself by listening and waiting for the silence

(Bollnow, 1982) that signaled oral completion before moving on to another topic, either mine or the students'.

What seemed evident was that the group discussions reinforced and highlighted the validity of the journal writings. The students read aloud from their journals, sometimes from each other's journal, and added comments that deepened and broadened the thoughts or ideas that had emerged in their writings. The discussions also allowed the students an opportunity to agree or disagree with one another concerning classroom issues. Because one of the major purposes of this study was to afford the students spaces and time to develop and hear their own voices, a consensus of opinion was neither important nor necessary for these discussions. However, many times the students themselves would make concessions to each others' opinions and would "settle" the fomentation of discussion, sometimes by modifying their original statements or, at other times, by simply admitting the validity of the other student's claims. Other times the conversation wandered astray, in ways I could not follow; on the poor-quality tape recordings, I hear comments muttered or exchanged that I could not catch at the time. I still wonder. My transcripts are full of blank spaces where meanings were exchanged subtextually and were coded language for their understanding only.

In addition, the features of the method of the research were as important as the method itself, as in feminist research as well (Hollingsworth, 1992). Perhaps, as mentioned earlier, Gadamer's thought that "emancipation is attained in and through conversation" (1992, p. 289), is a romantic idealization of language that refuses to tie itself to a single meaning for scrutiny. Actually, to problematize the concept of "emancipation" necessarily precludes an attempt to succeed in securing such a state. Words refuse to stay in place, to yield a static definition, to disclose meaning.

Another difficulty in the methodology is the student-teacher relationship that includes a tension between the wishes of the teacher and those of the student. Furthermore, as Britzman (1998) cogently instructs that "Any notion of education depends upon a theory of knowledge, but ... such a theory must begin within the tensions exercised when the knowledge offered through pedagogy meets the knowledge brought to pedagogy" (p. 5). Here teacher knowledge meets student knowledge, in patterns of subsumed and unconscious desire, will, and expectation, to become somewhat altered in unrecognizable form. What she terms "education as psychic event" complicates the notion that education is more than a contested battle for acquiring absolute knowledge and progress toward solving the issues of power, authority, and agency, but also one that seeks those places of recognition and awareness.

Thus, the focus was upon voicing perception of experience rather than determining whose "opinion" was more valid or accurate. Again, the focus lay in uncovering the differences in students' perceptions rather than in narrowing the individual perspectives to commonalities which sometimes conflate the particularities of experience with a larger whole. However, commonalities, to be discussed throughout the sections of this chapter, emerged as well as the "differences."

Transcripts were made of the research participants' journal writings and also of the tape-recorded oral discussions. These transcripts were further discussed for interpretation of meaning in hermeneutic conversations held during the fall and spring semesters of the 1993-94 school year. These later meetings, held as I worked with the thematization and coding of the journal writings and transcripts of the oral discussions, to create a preliminary interpretation of text, helped formulate, validate, and modify the direction of the reported results of the research project. Chapter 6 offers interpretation of written responses to a final series of questions and individual interviews after the deaths of two of the group members, friends of all throughout their years of school.

The writings and subsequent re-writings that emerged from the initial and later group and individual discussions were coded for thematic interpretation under five general categories:

- conversations about subject matter,
- conversations about learning needs,
- conversations about how teachers teach,
- conversations about relationships with teachers, and
- conversations about self.

In addition, subsumed under these categories of conversations are the themes of *desires* and *distancing* that seemed to be parts of a recurring, patterned path that wandered in-and-out from one category to another. Indeed, the five categories were fluid ones that were as interrelated as the lived experiences of the school day itself.

To be further developed in the following five sections of categorical conversations are themes of desire: on the part of the students that the world, lived life, and the teachers' lived experiences be presenced more and be brought closer to schooling; and, also, the desire of many students that they learn from and be taught by the teacher. The discussion of the thematic presence of distancing will include a consideration of teachers' methods of presenting subject matter to the student, of the self-perceived needs and interests of the research participants, and of the relationship between the student and the teachers as well as the relationship between the student and others. As we discussed the evidences of distancing found in an initial interpretation of student texts, the participants discovered and discussed an additional distance between the teacher's interest in the subject matter and the methods of presentation in the classroom.

The Child and Curriculum: The Contents of Life

The research participants began the study by writing about the classes in which they were enrolled during the 1992-93 school year, "the advertised menu," cogently critiqued by Eisner (1985). After defining the different subjects, the students ranked each class in order of importance. The third day the topic dealt with what was lacking or needed in their course of studies. All of the ninth grade students, members of my English I and Spanish I classes, were enrolled in a homogeneous schedule: English I, civics, physical science, Spanish I, math (either Algebra I or geometry), and physical education (a regular physical education class, varsity football, golf, or tennis). Most of the participants wrote very brief descriptions of each subject, limiting themselves to a sentence or two for each one. In linear form, they arranged their classes hour by hour down the page of paper in their journals, numbering each and underlining the subject name. The students, in succinct manner blended three strands of analysis:

- What a particular subject encompassed: "why everything in the world happens," "an in depth look at our government," "study of laws," "sentence structure";
- What activities were performed in that class: "taking notes," "sleeping," "studying for another class," "writing";
- How the student evaluated the class: "practice in trying to see around teacher's head while listening to the yells of bonus points slipping away," "important to pass because when I get a job I will probably use it," "difficult and challenging."

Interesting and recurring in this heuristic writing to introduce the research participants to the process of dialoguing with themselves and each other about their school lives were the numerous references to *life*. As the word reappeared in various journal entries, I turned toward a consideration of the desire on the part of the students to connect their learning with the world outside of the classroom and school building as well as prepare them for future economic or academic needs.

While English is defined as "learn(ing) about life, to think, to communicate" (journal, 8 March 1993), John claims that baseball is the "closest thing to the game of life." John actually defines the subjects that he ranks the highest in terms of their relation to life. Carl claims that the physical education class, in which he practices varsity football, helps him connect with nature and "in a way teaches me about life a little more than civics" (journal, 8 March 1993). Alicia rates her classes in order of importance: "I feel Algebra and English tie. I can't decide which is more important. I will use both of these the rest of my life." Cautious and thoughtful

Alicia labors over the decision of ranking the subjects in order of utilitarian importance. Breaking the self-imposed tie, she finally places English as the most important subject, perhaps because she realizes the importance in her life of her own reading. An avid reader, she checked out most of the paperback editions of adolescent fiction kept on the classroom library shelves in the course of the school year.

These students are not only concerned about learning subject matter that would meet the needs of their future lives. Several make reference to "the game of life." In our sports-oriented culture, perhaps it is not surprising that some male students express a metaphor of life as a game to be played and won. Just as Carl mentioned that varsity football and baseball taught him about life more so than did civics, Jimmy writes, "I realize I'm going out on a limb saying this since it's not academic, but you learn more about life and how to live wisely in one week (in baseball) than you do in one year of regular school classes." Mark (journal, 9 March 1993) quotes the coach as telling the students that "the closest (way) to the game of life is through sports."

As commonsense would seem to dictate in a male-oriented society closely controlled by violent and combative sports, coaches seemed to have the most influence over the male participants on the sports field; however, several are criticized as being poor classroom teachers. Unlike these students, I am uneasy about a prevailing view of life as a competition with opposing players whose sole objective is to win; the female participants do not make this connection. At any rate, Jimmy's desire to learn to live wisely through learning the "rules" of the game and playing accordingly may not be as prevalent a life lesson as less worthy ones. I read myself into his text here, intertextual, so to speak, textual hegemony, Britzman's (1998) "interference."

Significant about the recurrence of the word *life* in these writings is perhaps not necessarily what learning to play baseball or football teaches the student about living a life but that the student realizes that more is being taught than simply the rules and skills of playing a sport; furthermore, the students appreciate and value the correlations between learning and life. Somehow the teaching and learning, at least in these nonacademic areas, serve a larger purpose, one that connects, rather than severs, these male students to life. In addition to thinking about how a mastery of the subject matter will benefit them in the future and about how this knowledge illustrates connections to "learning" life itself, the participants felt a more immediate desire to learn subject matter that was relevant to the present, an expression of Dewey's thought that "Education is life." Almost as if he realizes that four years of an academic program do not generate the ability to make and implement daily lived decisions, in similar fashion to Eisner's (1985) complaint of compliant behavior fostered by schools, Jimmy points out the necessity of students' learning how to be more independent in some of his writings.

Ryan, (journal, 10 March 1993), extremely bright yet unchallenged by his daily schedule, makes a plea for "educational field trips that would take us to art museums so we will have visual aids to what we have learned. This would be part of our education as much as sitting in the classroom would." Again, there is a desire that the world be brought closer to the classroom, a more vivid world of colors and images. Historically, students have been portrayed as reluctant participants or players in the educational game (McNeil, 1988; Johnson & Nelson, 1989; Goodlad, 1983). Schempp, Sparkes, and Templin (1993) found that the teachers involved in their study did not find students wanting an education. This seems to be the general impression, the conventional wisdom, of students held by many in the general public as well as in educational fields.

As a classroom teacher, I, too, unfortunately have taught a portion of "unmovable" students. I have no doubt that this study done with another group of students could possibly result in different thematic distinctions. As a researcher, this rich possibility of "differences" posits probabilities of innumerable patterns of study findings. Nevertheless, in this study, I found a strong desire on the part of the research participants that they learn and be taught, one that they assert strongly in later sessions to consider preliminary interpretations of text. As we shall see, the consequences were dire and stressful when the students felt that they were not being "taught" or that they were being "mis-taught."

School and Society: Expectations of Life

If we accept along with van Manen (1990) that desire is not simply a psychological state, but also a state of being which signals a deep interest in an aspect of life, then we recapture the original meaning of the word desire which allows one "to expect from the stars" (van Manen, 1990, p. 79). The attentiveness of these research participants to the needs of their educational lives focused on their longing to integrate their school-lives with the whole of their lived experiences. Some write of things that are "missing" from coursework while others comment on "getting off easy" and "routine paperwork." Others complained about the replication of course content from year to year and "having to teach yourself." The constant repetition of remarks concerning poor pedagogy led me to think that students do indeed have an awareness of teacher effectiveness and realize their need for better teaching.

The *desire* to learn academic subjects more deeply, as expressed by Mark, is reinforced by Alicia's comment that "routine paperwork" be eliminated. She calls for "more of each subject" and "more" physical education for girls that equals the variety of athletic course offerings for boys. Perhaps if girls were offered the spectrum of athletic courses that boys are provided, the female participants would also speak of connections between sports and life. The automatic, subconscious link between the game of sports and the game of life is (un)presenced in the comments of the girls.

Emma realizes that the content of subject matter is repeated yearly. Not only is there a lack of "more," but a yearly presentation of the "same." The personal surfaces as Will calls for students' being treated as "people" and not "subjects." Finally, Veronica pleads for teachers to teach, rather than forcing the students to teach themselves by practicing a do-nothing pedagogy as her civics teacher seems to do.

In the first group discussion, when I attempted to deepen and broaden the students' brief definitions of subject matter from the first day's journal writing, the students instead turned the discussion to a rather energetic exchange of statements about which teachers actually taught. Seemingly, the importance of the teacher to learning superseded the significance of the subject matter to the students. Rather than discussing the content and format of each subject matter, other than to claim the yearly repetition of factual material, the students spontaneously exchanged views about which teacher did what during the course of a class period. In other words, the students' concern was how teachers teach. Whether we consider these writings and sayings in light of Grumet's (1992) "authority of knowledge" or Britzman's (1998) "interference" or Ellsworth's "mode of address" (1997) may be a matter of preference, a matter of perception, a matter of pedagogical practice. Of course, as teacher, I wrote the topics, I led the discussions, I transcribed the taped recordings, I read and pondered the data, I made the conclusions, I wrote these words. The complications of the discourse are written on each page, evidenced in every conclusion.

By the Book: Paradoxical Pedagogy of Despair and Desire

How do teachers teach? How do students learn? Are these such different pedagogical moments that they can be separated as binaries? Of course not. Ellsworth (1997, p. 139) complicates these moments of learning and teaching by explaining that

- The unconscious makes teaching impossible, and yet we teach and we learn.
- The teacher's 'authority' lies in textual knowledge—and yet she has no mastery over it: Textual knowledge knows but does not know what it knows (according to Felman, 1987, p. 92).

- The only 'instructive' form of self-reflection doesn't reflect the self at all. It returns to the self but does not meet the self; it's self-subversive (according to Felman, 1987, p. 60).
- Teaching about and across social and cultural difference is not about bridging our differences and joining us together in understanding, it's about engaging in the ongoing production of culture in a way that returns yet another difference.

Calling these complications the "fecundity" of teaching rather than a form of "nihilism," Ellsworth celebrates these "paradoxes and ironies" because it unsettles the notion of student and teacher and allows for work to be done in the spaces-between and spaces-amongst teacher as teacher, teacher as student, student as student, and student as teacher. The roles slip around in classroom practice and methodology as the undecidable nature of knowledge, teaching, and learning bump against each other and move toward new ways of continual and continuous being in that classroom. She affirms the deconstructive project to consider "teaching (as) a continuing and never finished moment of affirming and engaging in ongoing cultural production" (p. 141).

What, then, goes on in classrooms? This is a question asked by Sirotnik (1988) in a study of the data accumulated in his study of over 1,000 elementary and secondary classrooms. Teacher talk seems a simplistic finding, but one that is valid and supported by numerous other researchers, either anecdotal or statistical in nature, that Sirotnik considered while conducting his own work. He goes on to propose an educational practice that is more democratic in opposition to current policies that simply call for more rigid delivery and assessment of content that calls for teachers to "stand and deliver." So, in light of Ellsworth's celebration of the "paradoxes" of teaching and learning and Sirotnik's empirical look at how curriculum is presented in schools, can this research group offer us their version of reality? How do they see their teachers as teachers, themselves as students?

In a taped discussion (26 March 1993), Will, Chris, Emma, and I talked about possible topics for later journal writings. The students felt that the three days of writing about the same class period (in first person pronoun, third person pronoun, and then analysis of the differences in viewpoint) were too similar. Will suggested writing about something besides school, which I explained might detract from our purpose of trying to find out what school is like from the students' viewpoints. Of note to educators who see students as passive recipients of education is the fact that Will did indeed in some of his journal entries take the assigned topic and relate the idea of the writing to a broader realm of experience, of his own creation, and, at the same time, capture the flavor of the assignment. Here is an in-between movement between teacher direction and student agency. Rich and invigorating.

However, during this brief exchange of remarks negotiating writing topics, Emma, in a loud voice, interrupted the discussion with a disclaimer about how "really bad" teachers are. Stating that they "can learn more from people than from books," most join in with claims that teachers just use the textbook as a crutch, adding little or no content from other sources. Seemingly, these students perceive their teachers as teaching from rote "by heart" directly from a textbook rather than teaching in a broader manner that includes additional knowledge gained from either lived or academic experience or from the affective, "how they feel about things." The desire to gain that direct contact with a teacher's knowledge, feelings, and experiences calls for the teacher to broaden the knowledge base of classroom teaching to include the whole person and a whole life, both the teacher's and the students'. Will's insistence that the teacher "get out of the book" is compelling and challenging. That these students were not engaged by activities or learning that simply repeated what they could read for themselves indicates a pedagogically embarrassing lesson plan.

In later discussions of preliminary text interpretation (15 December 1993), the participants pointed out the distancing between teacher interest and the subject matter. John, who calls himself "son of a salesman," who often writes using business analogies, rather vividly challenged anyone to buy a product from a salesman who did not believe in or care about that product. That morning, John suddenly assumed a wide-legged stance of authority in front of our circled chairs and demanded whether we would buy a tombstone from his father if he half heartedly presented the worth of the monument. Yet, the teachers, John claims, present subject matter with little or no apparent interest in the "product." Van Manen (1991) asks:

> What happens when we fail to understand that there exists a primordial connection between learning and interest? In schools and classrooms where learning now must be pushed in the absence of interest, one replaces the intrinsic power of desire and interest with the extrinsic motivation of hidden seduction or coercive compulsion. (p. 197)

John, who can learn in classes where the teacher simply makes a reading assignment and then retreats behind his desk to read sports magazines, wisely asks how a teacher can inspire interest in a subject matter for which the teacher himself has no evidenced passion. I think that he asks not for himself but for countless others who are not so self-motivated and self-directed as he in the quest for learning. Not only do we see evidence of student valuing of new material but also in Veronica's writing, the desire to presence the outside world in her learning experience through learning another language and culture comes forward in her desire to experience the "new" and unknown. This view is reinforced by the writings of Emma, "I am learning the most in Spanish class because it is something I know nothing about."

In response to a prompt to write a description of how teachers teach by writing a scenario, placing oneself in the classroom, and writing a semi-fictionalized account of that class period, the participants instead chose to stay within the realities of the situation, the concrete, by giving an hour by hour account of the day's teachings. Again, a look at the particulars of the day leads us toward a fuller realization of the whole by offering a careful consideration of the defamiliarized everyday that, when put together, makes more visible the total.

While my teaching was characterized as hard, challenging, and demanding, Carl writes about "a lot of learning in a very short, short time," the students seemed little challenged by most of their course work, seeing little purpose in the dull routines of repetition. I received my share of negative comments, quite valid, that in Spanish I did not always allow enough time for the students to grasp the material; Carl, in a later taped discussion, claimed that I sometimes ignored Will's comments.

As a researcher and teacher, I find it difficult to write about how these students rate my teaching methods. I too fear to fail. Since what is most important to me are the connected teachings and learnings I experience in the classroom, to be made aware of my possible failings is painful and undermines my sense of self. Since I have left the secondary classroom for other educational settings, I long for those possibilities though I know they are gone, a terrific loss. Yet, what Carl did not know about my relationship with Will, the astute "golden lad," whom I occasionally seemed to ignore during class was that Will and I always spoke at the end of the class hour, even if only to smile silent good-byes, nodding affection. Too, he wrote me a tiny note at the end of the year expressing an apology for the distractions he so capably created for all and stating an appreciation for the learning we had accomplished. We, he and I, shared much in the love of literature, learning, and writing. I digress in the memory but add only that Carl had no way to understand that this was a gentle way to provide teacher attention to other students. I could have spent the hour teaching only to Will's creative genius, but that is a luxury unfortunately unafforded in teaching, despite the call for "differentiated instruction." Those spaces have to be sliced into millions of pieces. However, I love Carl's painful candor and his perception was probably shared and thought by others. What we cannot know is legion.

However, if I had to describe my own teaching during this school year, I would use the exact words as Carl's "a lot of learning in a short, short time"; I taught with the intent of broadening and deepening their abilities to read, speak, write, and listen as much as possible. I shared the sense of pressure, at times, overwhelmingly so. Nevertheless, a salient point of this conversation of how teachers teach is to show that students are desirous of learning and that they also have the ability and desire to determine the value and effectiveness of the classroom teacher's practice from their own perspectives.

Shor (1992) writes in a section titled "Students More Than Zero" that students have intellectual resources that they do not use or display in many classrooms but which can be brought out by student-centered and more democratic pedagogy. My experience of working with students leads me to agree with Shor (1992) that:

> They know more and possess more skills than they show in passive, teacher-centered classrooms; they can read, write, listen, and debate with more care than they habitually demonstrate; they feel more deeply about experiences and ideas than they let on, withdrawn as they are into boredom or defensive silence; teacher-talk, standardized testing, commercial textbooks, shabby environments, and dull academic courses have produced resistance and low expectations, depressing their levels of performance; they are on a performance strike, having learned to withhold full performance in passive schooling; they are brighter, more articulate, and have more emotional depth than the standard syllabus allows them to show. (p. 224)

Shor's indictment of the lived reality of classroom practice is supported by my own twenty years or so of classroom teaching and my observations of my own practice and that of other teachers. I broke that "performance strike" at times with radical progressive pedagogy. And too, students, rather than living as *tabula rasa*, to be imprinted with the sketchy outlines of learning, also seem aware of the need to do more, learn more, experience more, and think more.

bell hooks (2003) invites teachers into a democratic conversation of inclusion, of a cordial invitation of the outside world with all its richness into the mostly sterile school setting; of continuous and life-long literacy, of irenic power through mastery of the master's word; of progressive practices and policies, of demonstration and display of "joyful practice" (p. 44); of "radical openness" to "explore different perspectives and change one's mind as new information is presented" (p. 48). She cites Paulo Freire in *Pedagogy of the Heart* as he calls for happiness in the classroom, pleasure in learning, respect for freedom (p. 44). What a challenging call for curriculum reform that is rich, fecund in possibilities.

In addition, several students write of the need for teachers to explain more deeply and thoroughly the material being taught. Several students wrote of teachers who were "good" teachers because of their willingness to take enough time to explain the subject matter thoroughly enough until the students gained an understanding. This desire of deeper and fuller explanation of subject matter is the key to the students' frustration with teachers who lecture, give notes, assign reading pages, or questions to answer without an accompanying "talking and getting out of the book" that Chris, Emma, and Will discussed earlier.

Carl, during a discussion with Ryan and John (26 March 1993), describes school, "It's like you are going through a factory on the rotary line and people are putting stuff in you and then they take you out. I mean they don't do you like you are going to be put together by hand, they just, like one person at the time does it, an assembly line." The distancing of schooling (subject matter and teaching method) from the students' and teacher's experienced lives and the distancing of teaching method from the subject matter itself ("We never discuss science," Ryan states) lead to the perception of school life as a mechanized process that treats the student as raw material and the teacher as technician who unthinkingly "puts stuff in" the student until the student is "taken out," either completing the course or, eventually, graduating from high school.

Mark, the most sympathetic and most quietly frustrated of the participants with the difficulties of learning and teaching, wrote a description of his geometry class. He described the difficulty he experienced learning during class because of excessive talking and completing homework assignments he could not comprehend. Others discussed homework assignments they feel unprepared to complete independently. Obviously, this class was the trouble spot for my students. The question kept recurring: Why was this class so full of what the students labeled "chaos"? What was the cause of the conflict between so many of these students and this teacher? It was not that the students worried about their learning in this class, though they did, so much as how the atmosphere in the classroom led to such confusion—for those participating and those not participating in what Will called "anarchy." I started asking questions during group discussions.

In a group discussion (2 April 1993), Veronica broke into transitional remarks being made about writing topics for the week with a question about other students giving the teacher "a hard time." Veronica's own relationship with this teacher had made it more possible for her to learn in class. In the next section, Veronica discusses the underpinnings of her relationship with Mrs. Allen. The other participants also share their perceptions of the problem class and discuss their relationships with various teachers.

Students and Teachers: Conflict in the Classroom

How do students act or react in classrooms where little is going on, pedagogically and theoretically speaking, except paper and pencil tests, rigid authority, limp teaching. What would one expect? Obviously students can either be dulled to numbness and sit in silent expectation of the nothing they are receiving, or they can be stimulated to create for themselves petite diversions or calamitous outbursts of defiance. Of course there are endless combinations and repetitions of the actions and reactions of students when confronted with "bad teaching." Search school records for suspensions and expulsions for concrete evidence of "bad behavior" that can only be a logical extension of "bad teaching." This simplifies student behavior as a correlate to that of the teacher which obviously won't suffice in analysis of such figures, but it seems more simple-minded to me on the part of administrators and educators who refuse to see the relationship between student behavior and teacher performance (this term is a catchall for the myriads of teacher practice evident in the classroom). Perhaps the problem lies in the hierarchical structure of schools that supports the nature of the authority of the supervisor to the teacher to the student. If one finds evidence of teacher lack, it seems logical that the supervisor would be directly responsible for that lack. Naturally I don't think so, but then I hesitate to support the hierarchy either. Yet, we turn to consider how the research participants, the students, think about teachers and how they teach.

Jimmy, in rewriting an account in third person pronoun of what had happened in the preceding day's first period geometry class, narrates his experience of "seeing a volcano about to erupt." He cringed as he waited for the anger that preceded the chaos and anarchy. Again, Jimmy gives voice to the desire to learn as discussed earlier, but what is more significant in this section is the portrayal of the conflict in the classroom, the "chaos" and "anarchy" mentioned earlier.

Emma and Jimmy (group discussion, 2 April 1993) enter the conversation to discuss their grievances. Totally unsympathetic to the teacher's situation they blame her for trying to be "cool" or for not following through on her plans or directions for class activities. Worse are their statements about her refusal to explain what they fail to understand concerning course content.

In dialogues and interior monologues that were representative of conversations between themselves and a teacher, almost all of the students wrote lines filled with anger and distrust. Carl's humor allows him to write a scenario in which a coach delivers a "lengthy speech on the value of football" in response to his statement of planning to quit school and become a tax collector.

However, the others wrote painful conversations comprised of accusatory remarks ("You cheated!" and "Do you know you've only been here twenty of the last thirty days?") or ridiculous commands ("Write and shut up!"), on the part of the teachers, followed by protests against unfairness ("But, Mrs. Allen, we shouldn't get penalized for something another student did!") and claims of autonomy ("I'm a free man") on the part of the students. Mark, always worried about the possibility of learning or not learning, wrote a conversation in which the teacher refused to explain a geometry proof to him and threatened to send him to the office for his repeated questions. In the concluding line of his dialogue, the student turned to another student for help with the proof.

Shown thus far are conflicting relationships with teachers based on issues of unfairness, unreasonable demands, threats, and lack of willingness to "teach." A transition to the distancing that most students feel between themselves and their teachers is a student who more closely identifies with a teacher. Veronica and her query at the end of the last section bring us toward her demand to know why some of these students are so "hard" on this geometry teacher. Claiming that she treats her teachers "just like my friends," she acknowledges that only a few teachers have reciprocated her kindness. The relational aspect of teaching comes forth in her discussion of her feelings of closeness to and trust of some of her teachers. Stating a distrust of girls her own age, she perhaps has chosen to befriend certain teachers.

While even Veronica sounds ambivalent about how well she or her teachers can or do know each other, except for Emma who writes about being able to talk to her Algebra II teacher, she is the only student who felt an awareness of teachers as human beings and who felt that her teachers realized her humanity. We remember that earlier Emma asked that teachers bring the personal into the classroom in that she felt that students could learn from the teachers' experiences. Later, we will consider Emma's profound sense of distancing that she feels when considering her relationships with her teachers.

Veronica's question about the other students' volatile relationship with Mrs. Allen led her during the group discussion to tell the group how she had met and worked with this teacher the year before while working at the school concessions stand. In her journal entry of a dialogue with a teacher, Veronica also tells of Mrs. Allen giving her a headache remedy before sending her on to her next class with an excuse for being tardy. Clearly, Mrs. Allen is a worthy and warm person for Veronica on a personal level.

Emma, when asked to talk about her relationships with her teachers, tells the group that the only teacher she could ever talk to was Mrs. Leopold, perhaps, due to spending time in her home as a friend of Mrs. Leopold's daughter. In a matter of fact voice, reminiscent of my own ninth grade experiences, Emma succinctly claims that "That's just the way it is" and "It's always been like that" (group discussion, 2 April 1993). Other than sustaining a relationship through friendship with a teacher's daughter, Emma has little or no personal contact with her teachers.

I remember how surprised I felt when my geometry teacher called me up to her desk. My initial shock at a teacher initiating a conversation with me was only overshadowed by a cold shower of feelings of worthlessness, a veritable deluge, when she warned me that I needed to pull my skirt down. I sympathize with Emma when she later tells the group that most of her teachers think "I am a juvenile delinquent." Clearly, teachers have the power to evoke strong feelings in students with chance remarks spoken unthinkingly or hastily.

Emma, in an earlier journal entry, had proposed that while teachers are "people," most students cannot conceive of their actually having a family and life due to the lack of sharing of personal experiences. She searches for a possible connection between the student and the teacher through reciprocal knowledge as she writes: "It makes students feel like they are on the same level of the teacher instead of feeling beneath them" (journal, 31 March 1993). She goes on to discuss her relationship with Mrs. Leopold, relating that they treated each other as "equals, not a superior and a lowly student."

Veronica and Emma seem to have been able to forge viable relationships with some or at least one of their women teachers while most of the others mainly experience relationships of distancing. Carl (journal, 31 March 1993) writes that his relationship with myself "usually stays at the level of student-teacher." In unusual language, he claims that sometimes I become "a little rowdy and step out for a few seconds, but just as soon as she steps out, she is right back in." Somehow, Carl must feel that I move across some of that distance that separates student and teacher but quickly move back toward a separate teacher space. Alicia (journal, 31 March 1993) writes ambivalently about feeling "comfortable" around me and that "we get along fine," but also about having the idea that "I guess that I understand Mrs. B., but whether she understands me I don't know." Ryan (journal, 31 March 1993) goes the full distance in the opposite direction as he states, matter of factly, that "The relationship with my teachers is strictly business and nothing personal." Furthermore, he feels a lack of reciprocal understanding between himself and his teachers. Clearly, he is one of the most isolated of the group though later he states that through working with this research project he felt much less so.

The issue of equality as a desired ingredient of a relationship that negates the problem of distancing is brought up by Carl as did Emma earlier. When Carl claims that a student's relationship depends on the teacher's mood as well as the individual teacher herself, I counterpose his argument by suggesting that perhaps the student then who stays the same day by day is the constant in the relationship. Carl (group discussion, 2 April 1993) reacts, "Yeah, they don't care. Sometimes they might make the first move talking to you, but it just depends on how they are.... They don't notice how you feel. You can't just walk up to a teacher and start talking. But he can walk up to you." In response to Carl's proposal of teacher determination of relationship, I comment, "You feel a distance and you feel that the teacher determines that distance in the relationship." Though some of these students make tentative advances towards establishing a relationship with teachers, the power to initiate the relationship lies within the teacher's realm.

Thus far, throughout this chapter, we have seen evidence of distancing between what the student learns and desires to learn, between actual subject matter and life experiences, between teachers' interests and subject matter, and between teaching methods and subject matter, accompanied by a counterpoint of a strong desire to learn from life—the larger world as well as the realms of lived experiences. Though in later text interpretation (15 December 1993), Emma warns that sometimes a "business-like" relationship with a teacher is best, this chasm between the students' lives and that of the teacher may be the crucial distancing in the classroom—the removal of the teacher's life from those of the students'. Later hermeneutic conversations will reinforce the validity of this idea.

The Notion of Self: Understanding and Curriculum

How to consider self in light of curriculum? Caputo (1987, p. 29) writes about Kierkegaard's "existential theory of the self" in which this self is self-chosen, self-fabricated in a claiming of one's existence. There is no evidence of an element of permanence that allows one a timeless and obdurate form, but an element of achievement, a performative task, "a task to be achieved—not as a presence but as possibility" (p. 29). Yet, Ellsworth's paradoxes of teaching and learning as she writes of Felman's notion that reflection "returns to the self but does not meet self" help us re-consider, re-flect, re-construct the consideration of self as an action verb and not a noun. It is what we do, not what we are. I think of Neruda's poem about searching for himself and at every turn, every time, he thinks he has found himself, in himself, as himself, a stranger peers at him from the mirror. I paraphrase poorly, but the point is, should there be one, that the self is an illusive, becoming soul who lacks the balance to dance on the point of needles or the photogenic qualities to pose for portraits printed on fossilized remains of the past. Perhaps this is partial reason for the breakdown in reflection that we experienced as the research group and I met in recent meetings and found that how we had once perceived our experiences was inexplicably strange. The self had moved.

However, the last day's writing during the original project was a prompt to reflect about the previous topics in order to explain, elaborate, or to write about anything of importance that we had not touched upon. Carl (journal, 7 April 1993) ponders the value of reflection and in his usually bantering tone writes. "I even think back on my baths and showers in a way that I've never seen them before. It's like going under water and opening your eyes and looking back out at the sun or someone else looking down at you. Have you ever wondered if your mirror is a window and someone else is looking at you?" Obviously he would enjoy Neruda's version of self.

With a mixture of the absurd and comical, he points seriously toward a reconsideration of perception of self. How can we understand ourselves as teachers and students? What affects the move from the surface of everyday life to the murky pools of consciousness that barely reflect the sun's light or absorb the silent rays of the moon? Can we dive and then triumphantly emerge or do we lie quiescent, submerged with thoughts and memories? Is it possible to shove hard against the bottom of reality and propel ourselves to the now glittering surface to break the thin film of water that holds us captives?

Through dialogue, a conversation which evolved into an interchange and discussion of ideas supported by experience while seeking mutual understanding, the research participants and I voiced a collective and individual speaking, weaving a story of teaching and learning, of teachers and students held by threads of desire and distancing. Moving from the whole of the classroom experience to the singularity of the individual and then back again in endless interplay of voicings, allowance is made for consideration of self-perception. We speak ourselves.

I attempted to represent a partial view of my life in an earlier chapter where I discussed and described the details of the small, rural town of my childhood and the formations of my lived life: school, family, and church. I never felt or acted myself far in thought or action from this trinity. This tripod placed me in the world and outlined my spatial and temporal boundaries, my horizons. My ties to the larger world of consciousness were evidenced through learning: the reading that I did in the classroom as well as individual readings of literature. Through geography books, biographies, travel accounts, tales of intrigue and romance, I read myself into the world. I came to it; I approached the world in dark corners of a room and imagined that I could see, hear, smell, taste, and feel its contours.

I desire to know, to feel, to experience, to draw close to others. I "expect from the stars." I bring to the classroom an awareness of who and where I am. Ethical and moral concerns for my students underlie my teaching practice. I attempt a caring and critical curriculum. I demand that my students and I learn. Perhaps I do not have the right to impose my caring concerns and desire for knowledge on students who do not share or cannot share similar wishes. I perceive myself as a teacher. Alicia labels me "a teacher-teacher" (journal, 11 March 1993). Sometimes, not always, as I reflect with feelings of shame and sorrow, I am worthy of the designation.

Who sits in my classroom? Who are the participants and how can they understand themselves as individuals and students? When writing about how they added to or participated in our English class, most disclaimed the importance of their physical or voiced presence, noting that they contributed more through their silent writings. Emma and Jimmy claimed that their presence made absolutely no impression upon the class. Will made a deliberate shift from talking about his presence to a more abstract, yet prophetic, claim that everyone plays a large role in life and would be missed if gone. Later, he writes in his journal about the "missing tile."

Alicia ambivalently claims to "participate more in this class more than any class because participation is used more" yet, at the same time, feels that she adds nothing to the class but an occasional opinion. Ryan, more likely to laugh and withdraw, declares that "I don't really think that my presence means very much to the class as a whole, so I contribute by my writing" (journal, 29 March 1993).

Veronica claims to be "quiet" which signals lack of contribution to discussions and feels that she "expresses herself better on paper" (journal, 29 March 1993).

The businessman, John, declares that coming to our class is "like coming to work; you always know you will be doing something." While Mark, always concerned that he learn as much as possible, feels unnoticed, as well he might in this class of verbal extroverts. On the other hand, Emma and Jimmy, both of whom express themselves lucidly and vividly, often poignantly, in writings of all kinds, contend that their presence is null. Emma, like Alicia, sees herself as participating more in this class than in the others; yet, she still writes that "I think my presence doesn't mean much in the class; I'm sure it's no different when I'm not here." Also, echoing Alicia's ambivalence, she states that the reason for her "insignificance" is that she "participates so little." Why do students feel they are so unimportant? Why, indeed?

Chris and Will, who present counterpositions of life itself, one somber and melancholy, the other lively and blithe, represent the poles of negative and positive. Chris who claims to "provide the downside or you could say the Death Look" and Will who would have us realize "It is difficult for anyone to imagine what the world would be like without them" (journal, 29 March 1993). These best friends somehow complemented each other in their day's adventures at school. Will, dragging Chris along in accompaniment to his carefully constructed classroom nonsense, could make him smile more than anyone. How ironic that the two who most strongly presenced themselves left so soon.

Clearly, my efforts at providing opportunities for these students to present to the whole class material (fables, poems, descriptive narratives, oral histories, autobiographies) written for various projects as well as time and spaces for smaller group discussions of writings and pieces of literature were not sufficient to counteract the teacher-talk of their other classes *or* the years of desk-sitting. Again, we have the theme of distancing—this time between the student and others in the classroom. These statements about self, created in the context of journal writings, help me to understand the feeling of isolation on the part of students even when a particular teacher attempts to create an atmosphere of sharing and communication within the classroom. Whether these feelings spring from the state of adolescence or simply are the essence of self, I cannot determine. I realize that I find feelings of isolation within myself daily.

In addition to writing texts that dealt with how the participants perceived themselves within the context of the classroom, they also wrote metaphors for their lives. Gadamer (1993) asserts that "the particularity of an experience finds expression in metaphorical transference" (p. 429). Thus, in Carl's interpretation of a student's education consisting of his traveling a conveyor belt with "knowledge" being affixed to prior knowledge until he was a finished and packaged product, we see a consciousness of education commonly held by many educators today. If education is seen metaphorically as a factory, do the participants see themselves as passive products? More importantly, how do these participants see themselves, creating text as evidence of their power to make meaning of their own lives? The original Greek meaning of metaphor is "to carry beyond" (Kutz and Roskelly, 1991, p. 228). Hoping to learn how these participants interpret their lives beyond the daily schedule of the school day, as they appear as students, as they appear on the surface, an attempt was provided for an inward consideration of being. After reading literary and lived examples of metaphors, "My way of life is fallen into the sear, the yellow leaf" and "Life's but a walking shadow"; "Man dreams the life that is his/Until his living is done"; and "I am a gun", the research group labored to compose conceptions of life with the written examples of Shakespeare, Calderon, and a tenth grade drop-out student that were set before them on flat, laminated desks.

Will, tongue in cheek, chides, "You ask me how I see life? In five minutes?" After reminding me of his tender age of fourteen but claiming to be "no more ignorant than any other person," he writes of life as a vacation. "You had better ride it fast and hard because it is not something you get to do every day." He continues in this writing to express a desire for life, to seize the day, to enjoy the moment. He did. With his death, perhaps it is this loss of expressed joy that now diminishes us all. He shared with us all. Nonetheless, this blithe spirit, bound barely only by the bell schedule, had a prescription for classroom boredom. "When you are in a class, don't wish it was over, do something fun until then." He always did.

Chris (journal, 3 April 1993) paradoxically negated the literary examples of metaphors, advocating a more positive view of life, surprisingly relating the importance and significance of life, in and of itself. So, for Chris, the self-proclaimed giver of the Death look, living life was the challenge of searching for and finding a personal reason for being alive. This is, perhaps, his final lesson for us all.

Emma and Veronica share a view of life characterized as a challenge. Veronica determines religious belief as underlying cause of her pragmatic thought that "Challenges are only temporary and so is life." Emma, on the other hand, sees the challenges of life more as valiant attempts to survive the difficulties of everyday life to maintain friendships, hide from others her insecurities and keep them from "smothering" her, daydreaming of another life. Several of the participants claimed to still be in search of their personal metaphors for life itself and, indeed, were better able to write metaphors for their own experienced lives when we stepped closer to ourselves and closed the world out. We wrote ourselves out of the general and into the particulars of the personal.

Carl (journal, 6 April 1993) pictures himself as a stray puppy taken in by a student at school. The elements of warmth and friendship emanate from Carl's writing.

A generous giver to others, who offers support to my efforts in writing, in group meetings and in chance encounters, Carl sees himself in active participation with others. He is perceptive. Another metaphor of sharing and giving is that of Alicia. She claims the organic metaphor of rose, claiming to share love and beauty with others. Emma, too, claims to be a flower, but one not universally accepted and loved by all. She adds planting and care directions that warn of her needs for growth. While Alicia feels secure in her ability to give love unconditionally, Emma has need of care and concern before she can fulfill the flower's natural destiny of providing beauty.

Two metaphors of trees—one that is growing due to deep and strong roots which are tied to familial influences (Mark, journal, 6 April 1993) while Jimmy writes more darkly during a despondent lull that his life portrays a tree that has died but is still standing. Other warning metaphors include Veronica's saw "Don't play too carelessly with me because you'll be the one to get hurt" that can either help or hurt and Chris's ineffectual bomb that "barely ever explodes and most of the time just sits and burns until the heat is gone" move the students' perceptions of self from portrayals of human warmth, love, and growth to more dangerous issues of feelings and actions that point out the possibility of retaliation.

John (journal, 6 April 1993), who earlier in the chapter pointed us toward the need to more fully experience our lives, shows an awareness of double perception as he compares himself to a poster "looked at by other adults." Warning that while the viewers see him as a "fine young man," and "unknowing they buy me and hang me on the wall in their mind," John realizes that "they love to look but they do not want me, the real troublemaker that doesn't care what they think." He concludes by saying "Other people view me, but real people know me. They are sold with a lifetime warranty." Reminiscent of Carl's underwater mirror image, John's metaphor of seeing and being seen at the same time, presents only a visual surface image while he exists underneath. While some only see external appearances, others who are named "real people" have the ability to "know."

Remembering that Alicia labels me a "teacher-teacher" and suspecting with fear and trembling that I do not always live that role with its enormously overwhelming implications for teaching and caring, I turn to the last journal entry (8 April 1993) written by Will, the lived embodiment of the zeitgeist of the class, who could play and act, at various moments, the many roles of being: the serious, the thoughtful, the caring, the distracting, the playful, the rebellious, and the studious. He writes of a teacher who takes the time to read the inside of a book before deciding its worth, rather than simply gazing at the cover and making a hasty decision to throw it away. This characterization of a student's life as a book and the teacher's life as that of a reader points toward an interpretation of text that includes elements of a teacher's sensitivity, understanding, and the insight to act with "pedagogical tact" (van Manen, 1991) which includes the ability: to see a situation calling for sensitivity, to understand the meaning of what is seen, to sense the significance of this situation, to know how and what to do, and to actually do something right.... Somehow, insight and feeling are instantly realized in a mode of acting characterized by a certain thinking attentiveness (p. 146). I have claimed to have literally read myself into a consciousness of the larger lifeworld; I acknowledge that within the classroom the students are the texts that I study and interpret. Obviously, the teacher too is a text for student interpretation. The rarity of the above writing is that this perceptive student who himself was adept at reading the texts of others was also aware of "having been read."

Throughout this chapter, the interpretation of text has traced the evidences of desire and distancing. This last metaphor of student as text and teacher as interpreter presents as well as leads to an understanding of the student's desire to love, to live, and to be understood. The desire for drawing close to another human being flows through the metaphors of the stray puppy, the roses, the flower, the poster, the live tree, and the book. The distancing between self-perception and external-perception is evidenced in the metaphors of the saw, the dead tree, and the bomb. The tracings of desire and distancing flow from one experience of schooling to the other, from one of us to the other, in unending circles of knowing and learning.

The Final Inch: The Precarious Gait of Experience

These students who acted as research participants during this project faithfully recorded their thoughts on school, curriculum, teachers, and self in full accord with the requirements of human science research. In open and honest conversations, they worked through their ideas on teachers and how they teach as well as their relationships with these teachers. Their primary concern or desire that they be taught in order that they might learn how to live life was of surprising intensity. Their feelings of separation in the classroom from life were a recurring pattern of pain and alienation, feelings well documented in academic sources (Noddings, 1992, p. 2). Through our questions about school, curriculum, teachers, and self, we have learned that there may be no final answers or conclusions. In the defamiliarization, even in the understanding, of experience there is no possibility of closure:

I stepped from Plank to Plank
A slow and cautious way
The Stars about my Head I felt,
About my Feet the Sea.

I knew not but the next
 Would be my final inch—
This gave me that precarious Gait
 Some call Experience.

(Dickinson, 1890/1960, p. 416)

Emily Dickinson realized the perils of living life, the uncertainty of experience, the distance "from plank to plank" that causes one to walk at a tilt.

The close look and attempt at interpretation of students' perceptions of schooling and curriculum, along with a cooperative effort at textual interpretation of lived experiences through hermeneutic conversation, seem to make the researcher able to hear a polyphony of voices: some loud, some soft, some encouraging, some angry, some demanding, some quiescent. Though this research circle has moved in time and place, the endless cycle of school experiences continues to evolve. We change and are changed. Time and death are great modifiers of experience. The circle closes in on itself and collapses thought.

In studying and reconsidering the way I addressed these students, worked with them as teacher and researcher, according to Ellsworth's (1997) notion of "modes of address," I acknowledge my privileged position as teacher, as asker of questions, as writer of text, as leader of dialogue. Of course, I very nearly dominated every moment of the study, although I can testify to the gaps and chasms between my leading and the students' following, in moments of meaning making of their own, in their quiet, almost unvoiced comments and soft laughter, as they constructed their dialogue-within-a-dialogue at most meetings. Now, when asked to interpret the elliptic moments on the tape recordings, they stare blankly and say nothing. The ellipses remain. Some things cannot and will not be known, only in partial flashes of understanding and expression.

As we collaborated in hermeneutic conversations the second year of the study (see van Manen, 1990, p. 99), we came to realize that our group was not the same group that met last year. We were jolted from life to death with the loss of two of our participants—Will and Chris. From April to November we had moved through change and time, some of us from life to death. Indeed, we live our lives "an inch at a time" and the "precarious gait" causes us to grasp at each other for balance and support. It became evident in these later conversations that our project was not concluded. We continued to talk.

In the next chapter, I discuss the issues that arose from later meetings and interviews with the research participants held in late January and early February of 1994. In earlier meetings held during the fall, I had found the group curiously reticent. These vibrant and outspoken students were suddenly still and shy. Where were my students? I felt that I had lost all of them, not just the two. Stunned and shocked by the loss of their friends, they sat and looked at me from underneath lowered brows and creased foreheads. I felt the unspoken questions; yet, I too was silenced. We had managed to get through early drafts of preceding chapters and valiantly, they helped me think about the thematic issues of their texts and led us toward deeper uncovering of meaning. At least, they followed my lead as I looked at their texts as I modified that approach as we worked together.

In January 1994, I returned to the school for final meetings that spilled over into wet February, this time with written questions in hand. If we could not speak, could we write? The group of participants eagerly seized the questions I had prepared and promised to have them ready by the next day. I had provided a familiar assignment. They knew how to write. They could write. Sensing a breakthrough from the strong, stony, and solitary silence of grief to shared expressions of sorrow, I planned visits to conduct individual interviews. I felt they were able to speak of the meanings of the loss of their friends and fellow students as well as discuss the meanings of participating in this research project.

We wrote to address the following questions:

- As you look at this chapter of interpretation of your text, notice that we use the word "life" quite often. How do you think we use the word? What do we mean by life? We talk about the game of life, of closing the gap between school and life, etc. What is life?
- As I write the last chapter of our study, how would you like our story to end? What final things might we say about our experiences together last year? What has participating in this project meant to you? What have you learned?
- How could I handle the loss of Will and Chris in the last chapter? What would you like me to say about them? Should I write about what the loss has meant to me? What it has meant to you? Would you please write about how you have felt since the accident?
- What else would you like to say? I am searching for and interested in anything you are thinking now.

I include this list of questions here to lead toward the discussion of the participants' written and oral responses in the following chapter. The issues of life and its companion death, along with the development of a deeper understanding of self and others, came forward in the writings and the conversations as the most salient ingredients of their experiences as students. Also, as in common in human science research (van Manen, 1990, p. 98), some participants expressed the longing to continue the research. I turn in the next chapter to consider the shared understandings as tendered by the research participants, filtered by and through my feelings and thoughts, for consideration.

chapter **six**

CONVERSATIONS OF CARE: THE DUPLICITY OF EXPERIENCE

To be whole means to experience the presence of those who have died.

—William F. Pinar, 1992

Teaching is truly pedagogic if the leading grows out of this care that inevitably is filled with the good of care. Teaching, then, is a tactful leading that knows and follows the pedagogic good in a caring situation.

—Ted Aoki, 1992

We always live at the time we live and not at some other time, and only by extracting at each present time the full meaning of each present experience are we prepared for doing the same thing in the future. This is the only preparation which in the long run amounts to anything.

—John Dewey, 1973/1981

In considering Arendt's admonition that we "love our children" and "prepare them in advance for the task of renewing a common world," I realize that, as an educator, I fully expect that the young person, the 9th grader, the 10th grader, the 11th grader, the 12th grader, who sat in the cluttered desk on Friday afternoon, anxiously awaiting the release of the dismissal bell, will arrive early on Monday morning to resume the process of "renewal." This is the expectation "from the stars." We think again of what it means that we be aware that we are living "at the time we live" so that we are "prepared for doing the same thing in the future." We attempt to "extract(ing)... the full meaning of each present experience." We remember that John realizes that we "may know life by heart, ... but what is the point of all this if you don't live it?" What is life? What does it mean to live life? What does it mean to lose life, to lose friends to death, to continue one's schooling without them? Do schools prepare students to understand "the full meaning of each present experience"? Are students taught the lessons of life and death? Can they be? Should they be?

These questions now lead the discussion. Suddenly, the importance of the previous concerns of the research participants with teachers and subject matter fade away as we turn toward a consideration of facing school in the midst of pain and sorrow, in the middle of loss. We remember that, for Dewey, living and experiencing are one and the same, equal categories of existence. We find ourselves in the world. We live the world; we experience the world. I wrote earlier that Dewey (1981) speaks to my private sorrows when he describes experience as the "process of standing something; of suffering and passion…" (p. 63). What he terms the "duplicity of experience" acknowledges the precariousness of stability, the "trials and tests of ourselves" (p. 63). Now, I more fully understand this "process" and the "trials and tests," as do these young research participants. Gadamer's (1993) teaching that the painfulness of experience "lets us see into the inner nature of experience" (p. 356) allows a closer look at and exploration of the dimensions of the aftershocks of the loss of Chris and Will. The others are left to learn. The hard lesson of finitude.

Closing the Gap: Life in Retrospection

Fear no more the heat o'the sun,
  Nor the furious winter's rages;
Thou thy worldly task hast done,
  Home art gone, and ta'en thy wages:
Golden lads and girls all must,
  As chimney-sweepers, come to dust.

Shakespeare's lines from *Cymbeline* repeatedly caught my eye and held the darker thoughts that took charge during the late night and early morning hours as I attempted to locate and understand my own ideas concerning the meanings of life and death. As earlier in the research project, the research participants wrote concerning their desire that life and learning be brought together in the classroom as co-equals, now I found that life and death must share an uneasy and perilous position of focus of later hermeneutic conversations. Shakespeare finds comfort in death's removal of the person from life's cares and with fatalistic dispassion avows "The sceptre, learning, physic, must All follow this, and come to dust." However, I found cold and scant comfort in the "quiet consummation" of the grave. While Will's grave now lies in the midst of a country churchyard surrounded by the sibilant sighs of pines and ornamented by a plain granite monument with his name firmly engraved, Chris, for a short while lay unannounced, topped by angry mounds of ugly, red clay littered with the tattered remnants of funereal floral offerings until his family made his grave a more peaceful place. I struggled against the relentless reality of the loss and could not accept the "finitude" of life. I do not accept.

Ryan (25 January 1994) suggests that I tell how the loss has changed me. The others urge that we remember Will and Chris in this last chapter of our study because of their importance to our work together. Will (class journal, 12 October 1992) himself had written:

> Even though a tile is missing, it still adds flavor to the floor. Its imprint is still there even though it came up some time ago. The missing tile describes how someone's spirit adds originality and life to something even though the person is gone. I think just because someone dies or moves away doesn't mean we have to replace their 'tile'. It means we should remember their mark forever.

We remember their mark forever. This free writing done in the early part of Will's ninth grade year had captured my attention as had several of his writings. To work with a student who loved to read and write as much as I while, at the same time, joyfully creating major and minor distractions in the classroom was a challenge to my own creativity and patience. Of course, the student who wants to read *Great Expectations* could and would be finally forgiven anything by an English teacher. The joy of learning, literature, and language. I smile as I remember. At the end of the year as I noted earlier, Will wrote a succinct note to apologize for the entertaining disturbances he planned and staged and to tell me, at the same time, that he had learned a great deal in spite of the mayhem. Sorrow, I find, is only part of the experience; joy in the memories of the person's life presences itself. I enjoy memory as it forms itself of joy with its sister sorrow.

Chris, as mentioned earlier, was the counterpart of Will. If Will smiled, Chris scowled. If Will could joke, Chris could fold his arms to assume a sardonic pose of sullen disaffection. Only in scattered and scant moments would Chris speak to me of his love for his little sister and, even then, in stories toned by dark humor. I found myself making conciliatory offerings to his moods: a pencil, sheets of paper, extensions of due dates for assignments, silent acknowledgments of ability, written encouragement in journal entries.

But he and Will could be funny. On a trip to a restaurant in a nearby city for a Spanish club Christmas celebration, the two of them found themselves, along with Alicia, forced to ride with the teacher some fifty miles. The other students had quickly jumped together in cars. For only a moment were they nonplussed, quickly glancing at each other first, then Alicia and me. But, by the time we had traveled a scant mile, toward the railroad tracks of the paper mill on our way out of town, they had begun a sit-down comedy routine, projected from the back seat of the car. I wish I could remember their topic of humor. Never ones to lose the opportunity to entertain if only their teacher, of all people, and staid Alicia. I could hardly drive for laughing so hard. Alicia glanced sideways at me, her eyes filled with mirth, her fringed bangs shaking against her forehead. I smile again at the memory.

How had I changed? Sorrow modifies all. I found myself less happy, less optimistic, feeling diminished, powerless, less comfortable in myself. I had fears for my students that I did not have before. In conversation with Alicia (2 February 1994), I tell her how I longed for the other participants, immediately after the accident, as if I had abandoned them. Perhaps feeling Ruddick's (1989) "preservative love," I grieved that they must learn at too young an age the harshness of life—the name of its counterpart death. I mourned the loss of their innocence—their belief that life is forever, that they are invincible. They have learned.

They have learned. Alicia claims not to have written a definition of life (in discussion, she terms life "a being"), but she writes of what she associates with the word, "Life is something that brings each one of us happiness. We really don't understand the importance of our lives until something tragic has happened. Life is something you live day by day." She wrote of the possibility of it being lost or taken from one. The expression "taken away" haunts our writings and conversations. Absence. The first thing a teacher does is either a visual or vocal roll call to presence the students in her or his classroom. Who is absent? Carl, having lost some portion of his verbosity, succinctly concludes that life should not be taken for granted, less it be removed. In similar fashion, John defines life in religious terms and worries the notion of having to pay for wrong done. Ryan offers a more balanced view of life as having a purpose as we were "put here on Earth by God for a reason that we have yet to find out" (writing, 26 January 1994). Though he calls this life only "temporary," he introduces the possibility of "fun" if "you live it (life) right and make the right decisions."

While most of the participants think of life now in terms of its temporality and uncertainty and as given and taken away by God, Veronica conceives of life as "nothing but one big test," linking her decisions, like Ryan, to "right or wrong." Jimmy, too, steps beyond the fears of losing life to the challenges of living life. He responds:

> To me life is like a journey. You start off young, not experienced and not knowing the terrain. As you get older, you gradually get more experienced and farther on your journey. Like a journey, life has its ups and downs, its gains and its losses, but a strong person, like a strong journeyman, will travel on.

Clearly, though in difficulties of coping with "its losses," Jimmy the journeyman is locating the stamina he needs to learn from and endure Dewey's "process of standing something." He "travels on." Here, Emma's thoughts conclude the consideration of the meaning of the loss of Will and Chris to our research project and lives:

> The loss of these two boys has changed all of our lives. We all knew them well, and they were a light in everyone's life. Everyone loved them, and to have them taken away so early in life is a tragedy. This town doesn't shine like it used to. I think this loss has made us learn even more about ourselves.

And, so, even as we find ourselves in the midst of loss and change, a diminution of the "light," we yet move toward "learn(ing) even more about ourselves." Are we all part of a single light (see Chiari, 1975, p. 64) and does the loss of some diminish the solitary flame? What have we learned about ourselves and how have we learned? What and how can we learn about ourselves?

Complications of Self: Interpretive Narratives of Resistance

Ricoeur (1974) proposes that "The purpose of all interpretation is to conquer a remoteness, a distance ..." (p. 16). We interpret our writings, consider our conversations, mull over chance remarks to narrow the gaps and comprehend the relationships between knowledge and understanding, between the familiar and the strange, the near and the far, ourselves and others. Ricoeur (1974) discusses Heidegger's ontology of understanding that recovers understanding, "no longer as a mode of knowledge, but rather as a mode of being" (p. 6). How can one understand one's own existence? Of course we can only call for partial understanding, a small sop hardly satisfying.

Can it be that "It is thus the growth of his own understanding of himself that he pursues through his understanding of the other. Every hermeneutics is thus, explicitly or implicitly, self-understanding by means of understanding others" (p. 17) ? While Ricoeur's call for "self-understanding by means of understanding others" is a viable aspect of this consideration of the student's understanding of self, Grumet's (1992) "knowledge of self-as-knower-of-the world" also comes forward as a means of conceptualizing students' self-understanding. In an earlier chapter (p. 16), I had written that "Learning self constructs an avenue, a gateway, a means of possibilities of learning others." Only possibilities.

To complicate the consideration of theory and methodology of understanding *self*, Alice J. Pitt's speaks in her work *The Play of the Personal: Psychoanalytic Narratives of Feminist Education* (2003) of the use of the personal in the narrative in a problematic manner that poses a less transparent and transcendent methodological treatment of research data. Noting that "Ambivalence marks the use of the personal itself" (p. 88), she examines the gap between narration of experience and its interpretation. Pitt complicates the personal as moving from the notion of a linear, representational concept of self to one that "is constituted within a web of relations that includes relations of time…and relations with others, knowledge, and authority" (p. 89). Furthermore, her concept of the personal includes the thought that "it may be more useful to locate the personal not in content that reflects the world but rather as a method for observing how we experience ourselves in the world" (p. 89). That is the question—how do we experience ourselves in the world? What is my world like? How do I become a person in this world? How do others? What does it mean to exist here? Now? How and where do I locate my sense of being?

Pitt goes on to explicate the difficulties and limitations of using the personal in research in which the researcher must admit to complicity in determining content based on personal narrative. Not only does the researcher choose content, but participants choose as well. What is (un)said? Indeed, what is it possible to (re)late? Is there an absolute narrative of the personal? What and where is reality? That old question. Yet, I do not seek Pitt's "transitional space where inner and outer reality can be experienced together" since I cannot acknowledge "these two kinds of reality" (2003, p. 94), instead I consider the notion of a reality as a continuum that stretches from inner to outer and from outer to inner with continuous and sporadic flashes of connections that constantly modify perceptions and further developments of both. Perhaps our attempt to sooth our unease with what we think of as "inside" and an attendant correspondence to what is "outside" is a waste of time; though, of course, this is not what Pitt attempts to solve in her work but rather my own existential worry.

What to do with our resistance to knowing self, to unlocking the doors to our black holes? If one considers resistance in a psychoanalytic sense as a process of managing psychic conflict, I have a great deal of work to do. In considering my gaps and theirs, emergent theories of "reality" should poke through the density of understanding and interpretation just a bit. Those areas of silence I experienced as I wrote an earlier draft of the text should utter little gasps of presencing as part of our stories of schooling and being. What do we will not to know?

Pitt goes on to relate that "where poststructuralist theories invert the humanistic notion that we name our experience as we narrate it, psychoanalytic theories further unseat the authority of the humanistic subject by insisting upon the notion of the unconscious" (2003, p. 49). However, a bit later, she points out that:

> In addition to asking how we can represent the experience of others in our research—a question provoked by poststructuralist concerns, we must also ask how we can understand the experience of representing versions of self, both in the stories we tell to others and in those we retell as research stories. (p. 49)

The construction of self is a troubling presence in this study as well as that of representation. Resistance theory, though helpful in considering student (un)success, academically and socially, does not inform fully as students refuse knowledge of various sorts—about themselves, about others, about the world. As narratives instead of psychic events, research stories told by myself and students must be analyzed in terms of resistance as a defense mechanism and understood as always meaning more than they can say and never meaning exactly what they say. So, the ruptures and disruptures of meaning will appear or disappear in waves of words and wonderings and wanderings of text.

Again, Pitt's (2003) caution of the complicating use of the personal in the narrative signals an "ambivalence" of meaning that considers the gap between narration of experience and its interpretation. Her "web of relations that includes relations of time … and relations with others, knowledge, and authority" (p. 89) makes our self-revelations and self-narratives and self-interpretations almost too tentative to consider. Yet, according to Arendt, we are in the world, we are of the world, and, I add, we are of each other. All is lost if we cannot claim some connection to others. I cannot (dis)count the (dis)connections, but lose the prefix and you have another version of reality. I return to the questions of how do we experience ourselves in the world? How do others? What does it mean to exist here? Now? How and where do I locate my sense of being? The students' writings address these questions as they write about themselves and others.

Coming forward in the students' later writings is the idea that one cannot know oneself in isolation; one can know oneself only if one permits others to know self. Perhaps I had missed the subtleties and complexities of the reciprocal relationships between self and others as well as the agency of the individual in determining the movement of the relationship. What the participants' writings support is that it is not only that one can understand others through understanding self, but that one can understand self through others' understanding of self.

Jimmy (conversation, 28 January 1994) cogently suggests that "The most important things are the hardest things to say because words diminish the thoughts that you have." Odd that the word subtracts meaning from thought and surely we realize that it cannot always contain it. Such rich perception. Yet throughout the duration of this project, these participants searched for and used the words to push our understandings to the outermost regions of our horizons. In response to the questions—What has participating in this project meant to you? What have you learned?—the research participants wrote statements that pointed toward the development of a deeper understanding of themselves and others through shared writings in dialogical, hermeneutic conversations.

Ryan, always one to keep himself to himself, quiet even as we met in the later meetings, kept his questions (26 January 1994) for several days before completing them. However, he filled the lined pages with tiny marks of closely written script and detailed the meanings he had found within the project:

> Being involved in the project has made me think a lot about myself and my feelings inside. Prior to being involved, I didn't do too much thinking about much of anything. I've been allowed to express many feelings and ideas that otherwise I wouldn't have shared. I most probably would have kept it all bottled up inside and never actually gotten to know myself and others.

This lengthy quote from the most tightly contained participant points toward the possible value of such research that allows for the development of a student's self-understanding—if, that is, such a self-understanding is valued in the school setting and to whatever extent that is possible. I remember Will's poem:

> There was a boy who didn't tell what he feels.
> He soon lost himself and lost what was real.
> He created a new person that was not him.
> His once happy life soon grew dim.
> He covered his true feelings with lies. He let no one see him cry.
> Once (there was) a boy who threw his word in.
> If he doesn't talk soon, he will never find it again.
> When you keep something bottled up inside,
> You are missing some of the world's great ride.
> Let go and drop it behind,
> Or soon, to the world's beauty, you will be blind.
> Please learn to let go.
> Don't be like the boy and miss the show.

Let go. Talk soon. Dramatic irony posits that this student did indeed miss, at least, part of the show. Is our tale a tragedy? Only if we forget. However, understandings of self ranged from a realization of one's own position of vulnerability as an individual and the presence of one's inner feelings to, as we shall discuss later, an awareness of shared commonalities with others.

Alicia joins the conversation about writing one's feelings into existence by commenting, "There were some things that I felt, but when I went back and read them, I thought—did I write that?" She continues by deciding that in her writing she tells "who I really am." Who am I to say she doesn't? She guides me through her understanding of the writing process. "One writes, then re-reads the writing, and only then realizes the truth of the writing." I have taken graduate English courses that focused on just that. So, not in the initial writing, but in the later reading does the truth value of the writing appear to the writer. Alicia discusses the process undergone in group conversations. "One writes, then reads the writing, and talks about the writing with others. In this fashion, the writer realizes the feelings of others toward or about what has been written."

Carl (conversation, 28 January 1994), the underwater surveyor of reality and rider of the conveyor belt, my own surveyor, instructs that "You can't get to know somebody unless you read something they wrote. You yourself write your thoughts, but you don't understand your thoughts until you write them. Even what we wrote last year, we are just now understanding." Jimmy concurs by adding, "You need to see what you're thinking." The difficulty of understanding and being understood in a group conversation seems worth the labor as the research participants continue the exploration of the value of hermeneutic conversation in constructing an understanding of self and others. Veronica (24 January 1994) thinks about her role in the project, pointing to the development of the ability to understand oneself through allowing others to understand oneself as well. She nudges us toward a consideration of the reciprocity of understanding. Emma, also, thinks about the possibility that she might "show people" herself:

> I have learned that I'm not alone in anything. Other people feel the same as I do and they understand. At first I didn't like the idea of this project, to tell and show people myself. Now I know that in order to know yourself, you must let others know you. (20 January 1994)

While this sensitive and sometimes withdrawn participant expresses the necessity of relational knowing, she still maintains a distance between herself and those she perceives as not her "friends." Emma's observations bring to mind Stern's (1990) findings that, for adolescent girls, "Relationships without independence become just as problematic as independence without relationships" (p. 84). However, Emma does acknowledge the connections to self-understanding through knowledge of self by others.

The writings and conversation draw forth the notion that a person "allows" others to know self. One plays the role of gatekeeper to an understanding of Pitt's "versions of self" by others. One understands and allows others to understand, at least on some sort of conscious level. Yet, through the allowance, the permission to draw closer, one gains a grain of self-understanding. I find this a curious idea, somehow, one of which I had not fully understood the significance. Perhaps, this is something that I "knew" without "understanding." Furthermore, the notion of the reciprocity of understanding leads toward a consideration of commonalities discussed by the participants.

What can we understand about each other? What do we resist knowing? What do we understand about ourselves? Emma earlier wrote, "Other people feel the same as I do" and "I feel better about myself because I am not alone in anything." How do people feel the same and how are we not alone? Veronica (26 January 1994) elaborates, "People aren't as different as it seems. Sure, everyone has their own mind, but we aren't that different. I'm not just talking about just this group but everybody." If we are not as different as we might think, how are we alike? Alicia explains, "I feel I've learned a lot about myself and others. I've learned that we all have a desire to love, live, and be understood." Alicia borrows my expression from an earlier chapter. So, we speak each other. In addition, Veronica and Jimmy decide that we all care about the domains of friends, family, and self. Veronica, through a reading of preliminary drafts of several chapters, recognized her own desires in those of the others, particularly those of Emma and Alicia. Jimmy reinforces the idea by suggesting that "We all have the same basic beliefs expressed in different ways" (conversation, 26 January 1994) which include a belief in some sort of higher being accompanied by a love of family and friends.

Van Manen (1990) suggests that:

> In doing research we question the world's very secrets and intimacies which are constitutive of the world, and which bring the world as world into being for us and in us. Then research is a caring act: we want to know that which is most essential to being. To care is to serve and to share our being with the one we love. We desire to truly know our loved one's very nature. (p. 5)

Van Manen (1990) quotes Goethe, "One learns to know only what one loves, and the deeper and fuller the knowledge is to be, the more powerful and vivid must be the love, indeed the passion" (p. 6). The notion of care, and its connection to love and learning, pushes the interpretation of participant writing and conversation toward a consideration of what *care* means when we consider it as an aspect of curriculum and schooling.

Care and Curriculum: Pedagogical Reform

Van Manen (1990) links human science research to a critical pedagogy as he writes:

> The end of human science research for educators is a critical pedagogical competence: knowing how to act tactfully in pedagogic situations on the basis of a carefully edified thoughtfulness. To that end hermeneutic phenomenological research reintegrates part and whole, the contingent and the essential, value and desire. It encourages a certain attentive awareness to the details and seemingly trivial dimensions of our everyday educational lives. (p. 8)

Not only is the educator's attentiveness directed toward the "details" and "trivial" of our educational lives, but it is also directed toward the students and their needs and interests. The participants themselves point toward a love of and care for friends, family, and self. It seems that their notion of care is in accord with Heidegger's (1962) description of care as "the very Being of human life." Here are located the sites of their attentiveness, their care. When faced with the transient and tragic nature of life, the participants push these forward as focus of attention. The deaths of Will and Chris pull into sharp focus the importance of life, in effect, distilling the complex experiences of life and death into residues of love and care.

Veronica (conversation, 26 January 1994) explained the relationship between her sense of satisfaction with life and the personal and academic aspects of her life. When discussing her definition of life as "one big test," she related that the personal, her relationships with friends and ability to "fit in," was more crucial to her sense of well-being than her success in academic subjects. I expected the reverse, especially as she used the educational metaphor of "test." However, the test is a self-test, to maintain friendships and, at the same time, live according to her personal morals and codes of behavior. Veronica, the test-taker and winner at district literary rally, links her life to issues of caring for the friendships of others. School subjects are secondary.

Earlier in this chapter, Ryan spoke of his ability to now "think" about himself and his "feelings." Not only can he think but he can also "express" what he terms feelings and ideas. After having written these introductory remarks, requesting that I write about how the loss of Will and Chris had affected me, he admits that he has "taken it pretty hard." Claiming that it is easier to write about what has happened than to tell someone, he writes a candid account of his relationship with Chris. Speaking of Will who "made us laugh and really enjoyed life," he grieves that he could not "have lived it longer." Writing on the back of the page of questions in carefully spaced lines of evenly spaced words, Ryan brings forward the presence of his lost friend Chris, the sardonic one, by speaking of an experience on the tennis court:

> Most people didn't know Chris. He made me laugh almost as much as Will did! One day during 6th period, we were playing tennis. I discovered that I had pleurisy, but I found out the hard way! I was in the middle of a swing and the pain hit me. Chris was hitting beside me, and when he saw me hit the concrete, he ran over. The look on his face was very sincere; I could tell that he really cared.

Ryan, who carefully held himself tightly together throughout most of the study, finds a part of himself that he did not know as well as a realization of his feelings towards others and theirs toward him. Again, the word caring comes forward to signal itself as a significant part of the meaning of what it is to be a human being.

Caring, relational ways of being and knowing are not gender specific, as found in this study. Caring seems to be an integral entity for both male and female participants. As Jimmy and the others agree with Veronica that the personal aspects of their lives (the care for friends, family, and self) are the commonalities of experienced life, I now must wonder how educators address these issues in the curriculum. Can the care and love for friends, family and self, not to mention the larger issues of life and death themselves, form the basis for curriculum and pedagogy?

The findings of this study support Noddings' (1992) comments that:

> What is important to recognize and admit is that curriculum content—in the form of traditional subjects—was not a big contributor to satisfaction with schooling. Periodically, curriculum is touted as the key to educational reform and huge amounts of money are spent on its revision, but astute observers have commented more than once that a focus on curriculum revision is not the answer. (p. 2)

Indeed, curriculum is trumped by care. If traditional subjects are found to be of little contribution toward student satisfaction with the schooling process, then how might students be brought to a closer engagement with learning and curriculum, in effect lessening the "distance" to fulfill "desire"? In response to the problem of student alienation, Noddings calls for the realization of "multiple goals and purposes" within education as well as for the striving toward the single goal "to promote the growth of students as healthy, competent, moral people" (p. 10).

I wish to suggest that if educators introduce the ingredient of care to the recipe of curriculum to be mixed and baked as an integral part of the whole dish, then students might learn in multiples of ways to care for themselves, each other, the environment (local, school, global), and ultimately—learning. Not only can educators bring about "the renewal of the young," but these "young" themselves are capable of renewing themselves through a curriculum that is fashioned around their actual lived interests and concerns. Thus, the element of transformation is visible as curriculum is re-visioned as encompassing and being encompassed by the elements of life itself, the original "desire" of the participants.

To teach the student as a human being is to call forth rich and fruitful possibilities of learning and being. Such a treatment of curriculum would mean that students, such as those who participated in this study, could find a deeper engagement in learning and a love of understanding of life and knowledge. Indeed, Pinar's (1975) notion of curriculum as *currere*, which "involves the investigation of the nature of the individual experience of the public" (p. 400), leads the educator to consider teaching and learning as possibilities for deep and rich delving into the students' inner perceptions and understandings of knowledge. The students' movements and journeys toward self-understanding and understanding of others could be guided by educators who are able to assist these students along the pathways of growth and transformation.

Aoki (2005), in writing about "The Innermost Layer" of teaching, urges us to think about "a teacher's presence with children." I like that, "the innermost layer," the most inner, layering the inner, layering the innermost, like a flannel undershirt one's mother forces one to wear to school on cold days, an inner layer of warmth, fabric of care, clinging with a closeness to the skin that comforts. He teaches us about pedagogical care by telling the story of his wife June's forced expulsion from junior high school in 1942. Going to school just to gather belongings and return texts, the Japanese Canadian children were watched silently by their Occidental schoolmates as they departed. Taking a last look backward, June saw her teacher Mr. McNabb, "alone, watching us as if to keep guard over us in our departure" (p. 194). Many years later, after locating Mr. McNabb and meeting with him, June asked him if he remembered that day of separation, the separation of a teacher from his students. He simply said, "That was a sad day" (p. 195). Left unsaid must be the pain of betrayal, the betrayal of the "young" who expect to be cared for and taught, to be led into learning. The pain of a teacher in the midst of losing students. Unspeakable.

Nevertheless, Aoki goes on to develop two themes that describe what teaching is, "pedagogical watchfulness and pedagogical thoughtfulness." He describes watchfulness, that of Mr. McNabb as "a watchfulness filled with a teacher's hope that wherever his students may be, wherever they may wander on this earth away from his presence, they are well and no harm will visit them" (p. 195). That is the expectation, the hope, not always the reality.

I think of the last day of school that year of this study, the taste of freedom on the tongue, the urge to run down the hill in abandon. The joy is only present in tension with the requirement of returning in the fall. If that return is absent, the joy disperses in despair. I think of the Spanish club party I had here, at my home, the wildness of the students, my exasperation at the exhilaration and the lack of restraint, the expectation that the next year surely would follow. In my exhaustion I was impatient for the party to be over, for them to leave and take their youthful enthusiasms elsewhere. I wanted to clean up and collapse. Yet, I watched in faith that day, as they drove off down my driveway, that they would return. Some did not. Aoki writes, "Authentic teaching is watchfulness, a mindful watching overflowing from the good in the situation that the good teacher sees. … good teachers are more than they do; they are the teaching" (196). These words comfort my heart and speak to my loss. I realize that Ted Aoki would understand my longing for these students.

Going on to discuss "pedagogical thoughtfulness," Aoki complicates the notion of thinking to move past Western rationality and intellectual behavior toward the notion of thinking as "an understanding of thinking that might be understood as thoughtfulness—thoughtfulness as an embodied doing and being—thought and soul embodied in the oneness of the lived moment" (p. 196). In the body, embody, body in, close, gathered to the body, the soul, the heart, thinking as a body doing and being as one at a moment of life, a celebration of being. Mr. McNabb, watching his students' forced expulsion from school, my watching my students drive off that warm May afternoon, his despair, my hope. His hope, my despair. Embodied in the moment of pedagogical thoughtfulness.

Though Jimmy (conversation, 26 January 1994) assured me that the "higher ups" would not allow that the curriculum be changed from an emphasis on traditional school subjects to one that included moments of care, of pedagogical watchfulness, of pedagogical thoughtfulness, I wonder how such a curriculum might have affected my last year of teaching at this high school. He stood, shook his head vigorously, and motioned with flailing arms as he flatly stated the impossibility of a teacher's changing the direction of curriculum. He is right, of course.

Yet I wonder. I remember all of the students whom I taught that last school year—the lack of regard for self and others, the listless attempts at learning. This past year, the student body, for the most part, moved apathetically through the day, waiting from recess to recess to final bell. Even sports had finally failed to catch much interest among students or teachers. The grimy halls were littered with paper and filth with black streaks of gum smeared from one end of the hall to the other. The janitors daily despaired as they mechanically pushed wide, wooly mops across the debris. Many of the teachers reported multiple discipline problems, and the office staff spent hours wagging their chins in dismay at the lack of respect on the part of the students and the lack of morale on the part of the teachers. Some of the teachers openly admitted simply to waiting for retirement. Others dreamed of finding different employment.

These research participants, these students, exhibited extraordinary insights and abilities throughout the duration of this study. Though perhaps more motivated and academically able than some, I maintain that this type of classroom-based, action-based, hermeneutic research could involve students of varying academic abilities with fruitful results. This research followed years of actively promoting more dialogic, more critical democratic pedagogical practices that had as goal the development of teacher and student as active participants in the process of learning and teaching as well as the establishment of a community of learners; hence, this study is the culmination of years of classroom teaching. I reflect upon my work in the secondary classroom with some measure of satisfaction that I have attempted to act for the pedagogic "Good" of the students within my care. I feel that I have done my share in attempting "the renewal of the young"; indeed, I have followed avenues of self-renewal. I have come to realize how important this is to me—that I teach as well as I can with the complex implications of "good teaching." Van Manen (1990) reminds the educator that:

> To do hermeneutic phenomenology is to attempt to accomplish the impossible: to construct a full interpretative description of some aspect of the lifeworld, and yet to remain

> aware that lived life is always more complex than any explication of meaning can reveal. The phenomenological reduction teaches us that complete reduction is impossible, that full or final descriptions are unattainable. (p. 18)

To negate and minimize the self-congratulatory tone that I somehow express that mostly signals my passion for teaching and students, not my competence, I sadly state a realization of the full and futile limits of my attempts to describe the partial and wavering ways that students give meaning to their experiences of curriculum. Rather, I have struggled to work with them in dialogic conversations to come to some sort of understanding of how they perceive their educational experiences. In so doing, I have learned a great deal. In reciprocal fashion, so too have the participants. I realize and admit to the complexities and complications of interpretation and accept the contingent limitations of knowing. My own perspective loomed largely over the whole, an inescapable presence in the project. I acknowledge the "exercise of power" as I exerted my efforts to interpret, even though I claim to be guided by student voice. Many voices speak here. However, as I think about the ending of this study and the necessary moving toward the "expectation from the stars" that awaits each participant and myself, I am reminded of a description of place written by Will:

> The mossy pecan tree presses softly against my back as I look at the wide, muddy river. The fading sun glistens on the water to make the light twice as powerful. The sounds of boats are far in the distance. A fish gently splashes the water and awakens me from my daze. I feel the cool breeze blowing my hair. The sun is half-eaten now. The sounds of boats are farther away. They are then covered by the soft voice of the wind running through the trees. The sun bids me farewell and I hear a gentle whistle, the whistle of a mother who seeks the company of her little boy now that the sun is gone.

I celebrate his writing. Though the day has ended and the sun has bid farewell, the mother has called the child to her for safekeeping until the sun's rays return to illuminate the water with glistening light. The care and love of the caretaker of the child—the parent or teacher or mentor (Remember Telemachus's guidance by Nestor)—Aoki's (2005) "pedagogical watchfulness"—posit an "attentiveness" toward the well-being of the child. This "watchfulness filled with a teacher's hope that wherever his students may be, wherever they wander on this earth away from his presence, they are well and no harm will visit them" (2005, p. 195) reiterates my hope and expectation that just as we "love the world" and "assume responsibility for it," we also refuse to leave our children "to their own devices" in the dark but draw them close.

I cannot forget my desire and expectation, I repeat, that the child who sat in the cluttered desk on Friday afternoon, anxiously awaiting the release of the dismissal bell, will arrive early on Monday morning to resume the process of "renewal." This is the expectation "from the stars." Regardless of the difficulties of life and the pain of learning the "lesson of finitude," the desire remains to draw close to life itself and, with Dewey's advice in mind, "to extract at each present time the full meaning of each present experience." Thus, the distance is lessened as students and teachers are prepared to undertake Arendt's "task of renewing a common world." We have made and claim these meanings for only ourselves, these temporal and sketchy narratives that describe what teaching and learning are, Aoki's "disclosure that allows us a glimmer of the essence of teaching" (2005, p. 191). Just a glimmer.

chapter **seven**

A COMMON WORLD: CURRICULUM-AS-LIVED PEDAGOGY

We need to move forward to a communicative democracy.

—PETER MCLAREN, 1998

All interpretation is an exercise of power.

—SHAUN GALLAGHER, 1992

Such a realm of the between is a situated place where the difficulty resides. In such a situation many of us tend to problematize the difficulty and seek solutions that offer closure. To be so oriented to difficulty reflects a reductive understanding of it, for which technical rationality may be the most appropriate means of resolution. In being so oriented, is there not a risk of foreclosing too hurriedly other ways of understanding difficulty? Is it not possible that certain difficulties are openings granted to us, calling upon us to struggle in and through the difficulties, thereby yielding fresh possibilities?

—TED AOKI, 1990

I capture my initial thoughts as expressed in the introduction, beginning this difficult and, perhaps, hopeless work of writing about and with students of their lived experiences of curriculum and schooling, in the process finding my own. I wrote:

> How do I begin to explain my desire, my wish, my drive to write about students' experiences of schooling? The fear of writing and the distrust of language to convey meaning render me voiceless, speechless, wordless. How can I explain what I cannot understand? Where did I begin and where am I going? What does it mean to look backward and forward while in the quagmire of the present? How can I speak lucidly in the face of chaos? Does consciousness begin in inchoate chaos?

In this expression I think I am seeking and experiencing Aoki's notion of the "between." I reside in the realm of desire and the realm of the possible. He points to the "tensionality" of the world that is and the world that can be. The spaces created between the two offer opportunities and possibilities, that through struggle offer curriculum reform. Curriculum, for me, is the everyday, the special day, the mundane, the sublime. The ruptures between and within these experiences offer opportunities for teachers and students, together, in the classroom to learn themselves and the world.

However, in this study, I did not expect to learn so much about theory, philosophy, curriculum, schooling, students, and myself. I did not realize that I was on a journey without a destination, that the journey was the thing itself, that nothing else had any way whatsoever of accomplishing any type of significance or coming to any sort of conclusion, a journey's end. As much as I am trapped and tripped by the narrative form and live and write to trace the plot structure, am mesmerized and dazzled by plot complications, anticipate and predict the climax, relax and wait for the denouement, I have been forced, in my writing and reading, to abandon the project as unnecessary and undesirable. As illusive and elusive as this seems, I have learned to wander the borders of meaning, to wonder at the contradictions, and to weave my way through the complexities of being.

If interpretation is, indeed, "hegemonic," as Gallagher determines it to be, then perhaps I should, for ethical reasons, relax my grip and (dis)allow the task of finding some (meta)narrative, within which I can work and, instead, search for some sort of irenic project that will enrich and enable the curriculum conversation whispering to me in such unexpected and odd moments. Perhaps, as Aoki (1990) suggests, these "difficulties" can "yield(ing) fresh possibilities." I may give up the narrative project, the interpretative project, to seek the (im)/possible project. I seek.

The metaphor of a journey captivates me so, I find myself using it in teaching and hear myself talking on and on, yammering, without conscious formulation of thought. Odysseus's journey home from Troy, Telemachus's search for his father, Wolfe's journey through his childhood and adult life, Dewey's discussion of the "map" we give students instead of the experience, Halliburton's work I found in childhood about his travels to the seven wonders of the ancient world, my search for self. I have been traveling for years.

My use of the personal and autobiographical detail shocks my sensibilities, so much that I can hardly believe I would reveal so much, always a dangerous enterprise, one I fear. I journeyed bravely, and always partially, through my past, not only in this work but in a paper "The Good Girl, Mad Mother, and Schooling" (Benson & Bloss-Bernard, October, 2004) that I co-wrote with an equally brave colleague. Not solipsistic mewling, but collaborative effort to mine self for meaning, others for connections, and the world for a space to be, an outward expression of what it has taken me years to learn. Janet Miller (2005) writes about the purpose of autobiography as "a form of educational inquiry, to call into question both the notion of one true, stable and coherent self and cultural scripts for that self." That is the unsettling aspect of attempting to story one's self. One realizes that every sentence written is a weak, contradictory, and failing representation of the gaps between the public and the personal, the narrative and the persuasive, the political and the ethical. The "cultural scripts" put words in one's mouth. Then there is the unconscious as it lies submerged, busily writing its own version with a leaky pen that leads outward occasionally and bleeds into the acknowledged text.

The social, political, religious, and racial scripts that I speak were partially written by the early mentors of my textual existence, the European and American males, referenced earlier, through which I read myself into being, in partial dis/harmonic chorus with women authors such as Charlotte Bronte, Emily Dickinson, Jane Austen. These were joined in my adulthood, in later conversation with others as I studied, read, and wrote about Phillis Wheatley, Elizabeth Gaskell, Kate Chopin, Alice Walker, Maya Angelou, Virginia Woolf, May Sarton, Barbara Pym, Elizabeth Bowen, Margaret Atwood, all strong women writers who demanded that I hear, think, and act in the world as a strong woman myself. I have been mentored well. My struggle to exist and know self-in-the-world in some partial sense has been a prolonged one, one that collapses and reinvents itself at certain junctures.

Continuing Conversations: Dis/jointed Dis/cussion

I come now to the end of this study with a beginning. This journey ends with a brief and, perhaps, ill-conceived continuance of the curricular conversation with the research group as adults. They are in and of the world now, out of our care, moving through society in various ways, seeking different interests, yet still joined as a community of learners, a cliché now in this day of ornamental and oppressive educational reform. What have they been saying? What do they say now? How do they (re)see the past? We continue to connect ourselves through language that seeks and (re)seeks the past through the present.

Searching the original data for a topic of conversation, I was struck again at the prevalence of male dialogue. One classroom situation that was addressed, in a review of original taped transcripts of 1993, seemed to show evidence of more male participation in the original conversations than female. It struck me, afresh, that the boys held forth more often and more strongly while the girls in the study either said less than the boys or deferred to them. What new perspectives do these young women now offer?

Fear raised its ugly head, fear of being wrong, fear of ridicule, fear of failure were phrases provided in explanation, in hindsight. One connected fear of failing her father, her family with connected fears of failing the authority figure in the classroom, the teacher. When the young men responded, they quickly disclaimed the issue as a problem, made quite amusing remarks; for instance, one began with "No, on the History Channel, they were saying why the women teachers call on guys. They were relating them back to a tribal instinct to reproduce. All the research showed. ..." (male participant, Aug 10, 2003). At this someone groaned, "Oh, my god." It seems that our collective sense of humor has remained, at least and the practice of discounting feminist discourse, one I experience quite often at the university level, often facilitated by women faculty who defer to their male comrades. However, another young man said he wasn't really paying attention to our discussion, and the conversation folded and silently moved away. Patriarchy is alive and well in our group would be my tentative thought. The resistance to re/thinking, re/seeing gender roles continues.

As stated early on in description of the participants, only one female African American student worked with the group as we discussed and dissected curriculum and schooling. Another gap in the transcripts, a wide opening or maybe a hegemonic closure, was the notion of race. My critical theory notwithstanding, we had managed to ignore the issue completely. To enrich our conversation and complicate our discourse, I introduced the topic to the group for discussion. Veronica shared with us views from her own research concerning African American students and white teachers and the lack of understanding of cultural differences that lead to decreased student achievement. She concluded her comments with an anecdote about a cousin being held back in school because of her lack of knowledge of certain words contained on tests, words that "aren't spoken in her house." She goes on to say that "But it's expected of her to know how to read them, know what they mean, and things like that. So, in a way, I think it's not so much race, well maybe race, but more or less culture."

Another young woman, Emma, who works with troubled youths as a counselor, discussed the differences between her clients (her term) who lived in segregated situations and those who did not. Discussing their notions of "the white man," ideas held by their families and not contested by me, she proposed that those young people who had lived in more desegregated communities were better able to succeed in the counseling program. She, herself, was shocked at the racial isolation of many of them and the difficulties it led to. Another group member, himself married to a Korean American, lambasted the government for forcing people to label themselves anything other than "American." He opted for a national identity as a solution to the notation of racial or ethnic categories that, in and of themselves, seem to promote "difference." Now that he is a father himself, it seems he has a vested interest in the categorization of his own daughter, though he did not discuss it. I sensed the subtext of his argument. I am sensitive to a father's love and concern.

The discussion wanders to the biological factors of race with Veronica telling of her niece and nephew with a white mother and black father. She worries the legal category, her own field, of race as she states the fact that children take the race of the mother, regardless, and that if one saw these children "walking down the street, you would say they're black. Legally, they're white." Doesn't the notion of lived experience cover all of our perceptions and realities? We are just walking down the street and assuming a racial identity, in the minds of others, based on appearance. Lived identity. The personal, the autobiographical, the narrative, the descriptive, the affective are all categories of reality that signal one's presence in the world, that signal one's perceived being-in-the-world.

Ending Conversations: Subsumed Dis/re/connections

Later, I wrote these comments, "Impressions, how to write about this time together. I tend to go numb under stress; I fought to keep my feelings alive instead of shutting down and letting conversations flow by." I always retreat into the private when forced to the public, even at my own instigation. Nevertheless, I had an email from one of the participants who noted that I avoided discussion of the two participants we lost, saying that:

> I don't want you to ever hold back when talking about Will and Chris. It seems that you do a lot because of how you are still dealing with it, but I think it's been long enough. Think about it: there's a damn good chance that no one has had anybody else to talk with … it's an outlet. (personal communication, October 12, 2003).

That my numbness is connected to this painful loss, I have no doubt. My lack of speech signals an inability to allow those feelings to surface, to break through the numbness to a fuller awareness.

Yet, I go on to note changes in appearance, writing "The body present/the past body replaced." The physical changes were reminders of time's passing, the verbal exchanges signals of changed perspectives, and all were signs of the present and the past living in the present. I continued with "I wondered if the others were flashing back to the past. I know I stayed both places at once. The past always present for me. The present already past." There were pain and magic within, a strange dance of being, a play of forces within. Both dread and anticipation resided, in uneasy though familiar co-existence. I can only wander away from that loss and look for the connections within the circle of renewed connection with the other students who still look to me for something, what I am not sure. I think I represent that moment in time when the future lay ahead, shining, unaware, innocent.

Yet, I find myself today, working in curriculum, looking for ways to reinvent myself and my practice, working with graduate students about to be teachers in an alternative licensure program, in the process of becoming. For me, now, the project is to become and act as the teacher that will be able to offer some glimmer of curricular and pedagogical possibilities to these teachers-to-be. As I study the reconceptualization of the field through the works of William F. Pinar and others, I become more aware of the underlying historical, political, racial, and institutional factors that situated my students and me in a school setting that stultified and enervated our personal and public efforts to teach and learn. William Pinar, in the preface to Janet Miller's important new book *Sounds of Silence Breaking* (2005), writes of the "heritage that framed curriculum as an administrative designation." As a classroom teacher, I chafed most days at the administrative demands, at the lack of recognition of the critical importance of academic content, at the often-demeaning content of faculty meetings and staff development sessions. Could this be school, I wondered?

In earlier writings Miller (1990) discusses her research with teachers in which they "focus on the limitations as well as possibilities of collaborative investigations into new versions of teacher-as-researcher" (p. 94). I came to live this life as a graduate student. I only was able to survive my last years as an English teacher at the secondary level because I was mentored and tutored in the history and philosophy of education. I began to live and practice my theory. It was a rich and hopeful time.

This has become my task now, the tutoring and mentoring, seeking the rich and hopeful times, as I teach curriculum inquiry at the graduate level, living the "new angles from which to approach the intertwined elements of social, political, personal, and historical contexts that influence, distort, constitute, and reflect teachers' understanding and enactments of curriculum" (p. 94). The question has become how can I move past and teach through that narrow, technocratic conceptualization of curriculum, discussed so cogently by Pinar, to one that acknowledges the lived present and past and a longing for the curriculuar possibilities and hopes of the future? The reconceptualization of curriculum studies, one that must impact teacher education programs ultimately, in my opinion, is an active agent for curriculum reform, one that includes the notions of justice and equity as well as care. The ethics of reform can call for no less.

George Wood, long-time director of the Institute of Democracy in Education at Ohio University, now a principal, I believe, has worked diligently for years to make possible more democratic public schools in his state. Working with public school educators and others, he worries the notion that current reforms further disempower teachers and students, making this country more at risk for disengaging from democratic processes. He calls for the reclamation of a civic mission, "a pedagogy for democracy, the goal of which is to prepare independent thinkers who are committed to the public good and willing to act on their own initiative" (1990, p. 100). This retroactive, progressive call, one heard from many others in time past, is one that can fuel our efforts to reclaim the public schools and snatch them from the clutches of bureaucrats, fatcats, and neoconcats.

Again, unapologetically, I call for schools and colleges of education to hear the call of the sirens, the keening of the ghosts, the exhorting of the curriculum giants of the twentieth century upon whose shoulders we stand. We have been taught by the complicated conversation of curriculum that the purposes of schools are myriad, that the curriculum itself is political, sexual, historical, racial, social, international as well as recurrent and recursive as it settles into somewhat recognizable patterns of being and living, lived experiences of learning. Pinar (2004) writes

> The *educational* point of the public school curriculum is *understanding*, understanding the relations among academic knowledge, the state of society, the processes of self-formation, and the character of the historical moment in which we live, in which others have lived, and in which our descendants will someday live. It is understanding that informs the ethical obligation to care for ourselves and our fellow human beings, that enables us to think with intelligence, sensitivity, and courage in both the public sphere—as citizens aspiring to establish a democratic society—and in the private sphere, as individuals committed to other individuals. (p. 187)

Understanding, self-formation, ethical obligation to care for self and others, informed thought and ethical action, commitment to a democratic society and the well-being of others are all curricular goals that bear careful and serious consideration in this day of deform and denial of human rights.

Again, Janet Miller (2005) thoughtfully considers reform as she writes "situated school reform draws attention to how these processes and goals constantly are re-written within specific school cultures and by particular individuals. School reform is not raising test scores to establish bragging rights for politicians; it is the subjunctive labor of self-understanding." How to move from external demands of rigid and punitive testing measures to the labor of love of self-understanding is the major objective of the unit plan. This "lived" school reform is one that considers carefully and considerately the living, breathing human beings affected by all school planning, one that takes into account the juxtapositions of the public and the private, the administrator and the teacher, the teacher and the student, the text and the interpretation, the conscious and the unconscious, the spoken and the silent. This reform moves quickly in the face of loss, addresses death, loves life, acknowledges the future in light of the present and past. It moves to fill the spaces, the gaps, the ruptures betwixt and among the lived experiences of those attempting to understand how they fit in the world. Those students who need, those educators who care. And there is nothing simple in the telling; the contradictions and repressions free fall through the conversations, dropping salient thoughts along the way. Yet we speak, perhaps in faltering, halting, and wavering tones to what we only hope we can understand and that others will grope toward some partial understanding. We hope we teach. We reach for the world; indeed, we intend to be "freed by this knowledge to act in the world."

References

Angelou, M. (1971). *I know why the caged bird sings*. New York: Bantam Books.

Aoki, T.T. (1990). Themes of teaching curriculum. In J.T. Sears & J.D. Marshall (Eds.), *Teaching and thinking about curriculum: Critical inquiries* (pp. 111–114). New York: Teachers College Press.

———. (1992). Layered voices of teaching: The uncannily correct and the elusively true. In W.F. Pinar & W.M. Reynolds (Eds.), *Understanding curriculum as phenomenological and deconstructed text* (pp. 44–63). New York: Teachers College Press.

———. (2005). *Curriculum in a new key: The collected works of Ted. T. Aoki*. (W.F. Pinar & R.L. Irwin, Eds.). Mahwah, New Jersey: Lawrence Erlbaum.

Arendt, H. (1958). *The human condition*. Chicago: University of Chicago Press.

———. (1961). *Between past and future*. New York: Viking Press.

Bakhtin, M. (1981). *The dialogic imagination*. Austin: University of Texas Press.

Benson, K.M., & Bloss-Bernard, K.K. (2004, October). The Good girl, mad mother, and schooling. Paper presented at the annual meeting of the Bergamo Conference on Curriculum Theorizing, Dayton, Ohio.

Bernstein, R.J. (1987). The varieties of pluralism. *American Journal of Education*, 95(4), 509–525.

Bogdan, R.C., & Biklen, S.K. (1992). *Qualitative research for education: An introduction to theory and methods* (2nd ed.). Boston: Allyn and Bacon.

Bollnow, O.F. (1982). On silence—findings of philosophico-pedagogical anthropology. *Universitas*, *24*(1), 41–47.

Britzman, D.P. (1989). Who has the floor? Curriculum, teaching, and the English student teacher's struggle for voice. *Curriculum Inquiry*, *19*(2), 143–162.

———. (1998). *Lost subjects, contested objects: Toward a psychoanalytic inquiry of learning*. Albany: State University of New York Press.

Brown, R.K. (1992). Max van Manen and pedagogical human science research. In W.F. Pinar & W.M. Reynolds (Eds.), *Understanding curriculum as phenomenological and deconstructed text* (pp. 44–63). New York: Teachers College Press.

Caputo, J.D. (1987). *Radical hermeneutics: Repetition, deconstruction, and the hermeneutic project*. Bloomington: Indiana University Press.

Chiari, J. (1975). *Twentieth-century French thought: From Bergson to Levi-Strauss*. New York: Gordian Press.

Clandinin, D.J. (1993). On seeing in educational research [Review of *The enlightened eye: Qualitative inquiry and the enhancement of educational practice*]. *Curriculum Inquiry, 23*(2), 203–212.

———. (1985). Personal practical knowledge: A study of teachers' classroom images. *Curriculum Inquiry, 15*(4), 361–386.

Connelly, F.M., & Clandinin, D.J. (1988). *Teachers as curriculum planners: Narratives of experience*. New York: Teachers College Press.

Darroch, V., & Silvers, R.J. (1982). *Interpretative human studies*. Lanham, Maryland: University Press of America.

De Castell, S. (1999). On finding one's place in the text: Literacy as a technology of self-formation. In W.F. Pinar (Ed.), *Contemporary Curriculum Discourses: Twenty Years of JCT* (pp. 398–411). New York: Peter Lang.

Dean, A. (1982). A proposal for interpretative analysis. In V. Darroch & R.J. Silvers (Eds.), *Interpretive human studies* (pp. 101–114). Lanham, MD: University Press of America.

Derrida, J. (1997). *Of grammatology*. (G.C. Spivak, Trans.). Baltimore and London: The Johns Hopkins University Press. (Original work published 1967)

Dewey, J. (1938). *Experience and education*. New York: Macmillan Publishing Company.

———. (1973/1981). *The philosophy of John Dewey*. J.J. McDermott (Ed.). Chicago: University of Chicago Press.

Diamond, C.T.P. (1992). Accounting for our accounts: Autoethnographic approaches to teacher voice and vision. *Curriculum Inquiry, 22*(1), 76–82.

Dickinson, E. (1890/1960). *The complete poems of Emily Dickinson*. In T. H. Johnson (Ed.). Boston: Little, Brown and Company.

Doll, W.E. (1993). *A post-modern perspective on curriculum*. New York: Teachers College Press.

Edson, C.H. (1990). Our past and present: Historical inquiry in education. In R.R. Sherman & R.B. Webb (Eds.), *Qualitative research in education: Focus and methods* (pp. 44–58). Philadelphia: Falmer Press.

Eisner, E.W. (1985). *The educational imagination: On the design and evaluation of school programs*. New York: Macmillan Publishing Company.

Ellsworth, E. (1989). Why doesn't this feel empowering? Working through the repressive myths of critical pedagogy. *Harvard Educational Review, 59*(3), 297–324.

———. (1994). Representation, self-representation, and the meanings of difference: Questions for educators. In R.A. Martusewicz & W.M. Reynolds (Eds.), *Inside/out: Contemporary critical perspectives in education* (pp. 99–108). New York: St. Martin's Press.

———. (1997). *Teaching positions: Difference, pedagogy, and the power of address*. New York: Teachers College Press.

Erickson, F. & Shultz, J. (1992). Students' experience of the curriculum. In P.W. Jackson (Ed.), *Handbook of research on curriculum* (pp. 465–485). New York: Macmillan Publishing Company.

Felman, S. (1987). *Jacques Lacan and the adventure of insight: Psychoanalysis in contemporary culture*. Cambridge: Harvard University Press.

Fine, M. (1987). Silencing in public schools. *Language Arts, 64*(2), 157–174.

———. (1991). *Framing dropouts: Notes on the politics of an urban public high school*. Albany: State University of New York Press.

Franzen, J. (2002). Imperial bedroom. In *How to be alone* (39–54). New York: Farrar, Straus and Giroux.

Franzosa, S.D. (1992). Authoring the educated self: Educational autobiography and resistance. *Educational Theory, 42*(4), 395.

Freire, P. (1970). *Pedagogy of the oppressed*. New York: Seabury.

Froula, C. (1989). The daughter's seduction: Sexual violence and literary history. In M.R. Malson, J.F. O'Barr, S. Westphal-Wihl, & M. Wyer (Eds.), *Feminist theory and practice and process* (139–162). Chicago: University of Chicago Press.

Gadamer, H-G. (1976). *Philosophical hermeneutics* (Ed. & Trans. D.E. Linge). Berkeley: University of California Press.

———. (1979). Practical philosophy as a model of the human sciences. *Research in Phenomenology*, 9, 83.

———. (1992). *Hans-Georg Gadamer on education, poetry, and history: Applied hermeneutics.* (D. Misgeld & G. Nicholson, Eds.). (L. Schmidt & M. Reuss, Trans.). Albany: State University of New York Press.

———. (1993). *Truth and method* (2nd rev. ed.), (J. Weinsheimer & D.G. Marshall, Trans.). New York: Continuum. (Original work published 1960).

Gallagher, S. (1992). *Hermeneutics and education.* Albany: State University of New York Press.

Gay, G. (2000). *Culturally responsive teaching: Theory, research, and practice.* New York: Teachers College Press.

Gibson, R. (1986). *Critical theory and education.* London: Hodder and Stoughton.

Gilbert, S.M., & Gubar, S. (1985). Literature of the seventeenth and eighteenth centuries. In S.M. Gilbert & S. Gubar (Eds.), *The Norton anthology of literature by women: The tradition in English* (pp. 39–58). New York: W.W. Norton & Company.

Gilligan, C., Lyons, N.P., & Hanmer, T.J. (Eds.). (1990). *Making connections: The relational worlds of adolescent girls at Emma Willard School.* Cambridge, MA: Harvard University Press.

Giroux, H.A. (1988). *Schooling and the struggle for public life: Critical pedagogy in the modern age.* Minneapolis: University of Minnesota Press.

Giroux, H.A., & McLaren, P. (1986). Teacher education and the politics of engagement: The case for democratic schooling. *Harvard Educational Review*, *56*(3), 213–238.

Goodlad, J.I. (1984). *A place called school.* New York: McGraw-Hill.

Goodson, I.F. (1998). Storying the self: Life politics and the study of the teacher's life and work. In S.R. Steinberg & J.L. Kincheloe (Series Eds.) & W.F. Pinar (Vol. Ed.), *Curriculum: Toward new identities* (pp. 3–20). New York: Garland.

Greene, M. (1979). Teaching as personal reality. In A. Lieberman & L. Miller (Eds.), *New perspectives for staff development* (pp. 23–35). New York: Teachers College Press.

———. (1988). *The dialectic of freedom.* New York: Teachers College Press.

Grumet, M.R. (1988). *Bitter milk: Women and teaching.* Amherst: The University of Massachusetts Press.

———. (1990). Voice: The search for a feminist rhetoric for educational studies. *Cambridge Journal of Education*, *20*(3), 277–282.

———. (1990). Restrospective: Autobiography and the analysis of educational experience. *Cambridge Journal of Education*, *20*(3), 321–326.

———. (1992). Existential and phenomenological foundations of autobiographical methods. In W.F. Pinar & W.M. Reynolds (Eds.), *Understanding curriculum as phenomenological and deconstructed text* (pp. 28–43). New York: Teachers College Press.

Habermas, J. (1970). *Toward a rational society: Student protest, science and politics.* Boston, MA: Beacon Press.

———. (1974). *Theory and practice.* London: Heinemann.

———. (1984). *The theory of communicative action.* London: Heinemann.

Hardy, L. (1987). Introduction. In L. Hardy (Ed.), *The Husserlian foundations of science* (pp. 2–14). Washington, D.C.: Center for Advanced Research in Phenomenology & University Press of America.

Harland, R. (1987). Derrida and language as writing. In T. Hawkes (Gen. Ed.), *Superstructuralism: The philosophy of structuralism and post-structuralism.* New York: Methuen.

Heidegger, M. (1962). *Being and time.* (J. Macquarrie & F.E. Robinson, Trans.) New York: Harper & Row.

Hollingsworth S. (1992). Learning to teach through collaborative conversation: A feminist approach. *American Educational Research Journal, 29*(2), 373–404.

Hollingsworth S., Dybdahl, M., & Minarik L.T. (1993). By chart and chance and passion: The importance of relational knowing in learning to teach. *Curriculum Inquiry, 23*(1), 5–35.

hooks, b. (1990). *Yearning: race, gender, and cultural politics.* Boston, MA: South End Press.

———. (2003). *Teaching community: A pedagogy of hope.* New York and London: Routledge.

Husserl, E. (1970). *The crisis of European sciences and transcendental phenomenology.* Evanston, IL: Northwestern University Press.

Ihde, D. (1976). *Listening and voice: A phenomenology of sound.* Athens, OH: Ohio University Press.

Jardine, D.W. (1992). Reflections on education, hermeneutics, and ambiguity: Hermeneutics as a restoring of life to its original difficulty. In W.F. Pinar & W.M. Reynolds (Eds.), *Understanding curriculum as phenomenological and deconstructed text* (pp. 116–127). New York: Teachers College Press.

Johnson S.M. & Nelson N.C. (1989). Conflict and compatibility in visions of reform. In L. Weis, P.G. Altbach, G.P. Kelly, H.G. Petrie, & S. Slaughter, (Eds.). *Crisis in teaching: Perspectives on current reforms* (pp. 141–155). New York: State University of New York Press.

Kincheloe, J.L. (1991). *Teachers as researchers: Qualitative inquiry as a path to empowerment.* London: The Falmer Press.

———. (1998). Pinar's *currere* and identity in hyperreality: Grounding the post-formal notion of intrapersonal intelligence. In W.F. Pinar, *Curriculum: Toward new identities* (pp. 129–142). New York: Garland.

Kincheloe, J.L. & Pinar, W.F. (Eds.). (1991). *Curriculum as social psychoanalysis: The significance of place.* Albany: State University of New York Press.

Krell, D.F. (Ed.). (1973/1993). *Martin Heidegger: Basic writings.* San Francisco: Harper.

Kundera, M. (1986). *The art of the novel.* New York: Grove Press.

Kutz, E. & Roskelly, H. (1991). *An unquiet pedagogy: Transforming practice in the English classroom.* Portsmouth, NH: Boynton/Cook.

Ladson-Billings, G. (1994). *The dreamkeepers: Successful teachers of African American teachers.* San Francisco: Jossey-Bass.

Langeveld, M. (1983). Reflections on phenomenology and pedagogy. *Phenomenology and Pedagogy, 1*(1), 5–7.

Lather, P. (1991). *Getting smart: Feminist research and pedagogy with/in the postmodern.* New York: Routledge.

Linge, D.E. (1976). Editor's introduction. In D.E. Linge (Ed.), *Philosophical hermeneutics: Hans-Georg Gadamer* (pp. xi–lviii). Berkeley: University of California Press.

Lorde, A. (1984). *Sister outsider.* New York: Quality Paperback Book Club.

Lugones, M.C. & Spelman, E.V. (1983). "Have we got a theory for you" feminist theory, cultural imperialism, and the demand for "the women's voice." *Women's Studies International Forum,* 6(6), 573.

McLaren, P. (1998). Revolution and reality. In W.F. Pinar (Ed.), *Curriculum: Toward new identities* (pp. 354–376). New York: Garland.

McMurtry, L. (1966). *The last picture show.* New York: Dell.

McNeil, L.M. (1988). *Contradictions of control.* New York: Routledge.

Merleau-Ponty, M. (1962). *Phenomenology of perception*. London: Routledge & Kegan Paul.
———. (1964). *Sense and non-sense*. Evanston, IL: Northwestern University Press.
Miller, J.L. (1990). Teachers as curriculum creators. In J.T. Sears, & J.D. Marshall (Eds.), *Teaching and thinking about curriculum: Critical inquiries* (pp. 85–96). New York: Teachers College Press.
———. (2005). *Sounds of silence breaking: Women, autobiography, curriculum*. New York: Peter Lang.
Misgeld, D., & Nicholson, G. (Eds.). (1992). *Hans-Georg Gadamer on education, poetry, and history: Applied hermeneutics* (L. Schmidt & M. Reuss, Trans.). New York: State University of New York Press.
Noddings, N. (1984). *Caring: A feminine approach to ethics and moral education*. Berkeley: University of California Press.
———. (1992). *The challenge to care in schools: An alternative approach to education*. New York: Teachers College Press.
Olsen, T. (1972). *Silences*. New York: Delacorte Press.
Orner, M. (1992). Interrupting the calls for student voice in 'liberatory' education: A feminist poststructuralist perspective. In C. Luke, & J. Gore (Eds.), *Feminisms and critical pedagogy* (pp. 74–89). New York: Routledge.
Outhwaite, W. (1990). Hans-Georg Gadamer. In Q. Skinner (Ed.), *The return of grand theory in the human sciences* (pp. 21–40). Cambridge: Cambridge University Press.
Palmer, R.E. (1969). *Hermeneutics: Interpretation theory in Schleiermacher, Dilthey, Heidegger, and Gadamer*. Evanston, IL: Northwestern University Press.
Pinar, W.F. (1975). Currere: Toward reconceptualization. In W.F. Pinar (Ed.), *Curriculum theorizing* (pp. 396–414). Berkeley: McCutchan.
———. (1991). Curriculum as social psychoanalysis: On the significance of place. In J.L. Kincheloe & W.F. Pinar (Eds.). *Curriculum as social psychoanalysis* (pp. 165–186). Albany: State University of New York Press.
———. (1992). Cries and Whispers. In W.F. Pinar & W.M. Reynolds (Eds.). *Understanding curriculum as phenomenological and deconstructed text* (pp. 92–101). New York: Teachers College Press.
———. (2004). *What is curriculum theory?* Mahwah, NJ: Lawrence Erlbaum Associates.
Pinar, W.F., & Bowers, C.A. (1992). Politics of curriculum: Origins, controversies, and significance of critical perspectives. In G. Grant (Ed.), *Review of Research in Education, 18*, 163–190.
Pinar, W.F., Reynolds, W.M., Slattery, P., & Taubman, P.M. (Eds.). (2002). *Understanding curriculum: An introduction to the study of historical and contemporary curriculum discourses*. New York: Peter Lang.
Pitt, A.J. (2003). *The play of the personal: Psychoanalytic narratives of feminist education*. New York: Peter Lang.
Popp, J.A. (1987). If you see John Dewey, tell him we did it. *Educational Theory, 37*(2), 145–152.
Psathas, G. (Ed.). (1973). *Phenomenological sociology*. NY: John Wiley and Sons.
Reynolds, W.M., & Webber, J.A. (Eds.). (2004). *Expanding curriculum theory: Dis/positions and lines of flight*. Mahwah, New Jersey: Lawrence Erlbaum Publishers.
Rice, S., & Burbules, N.C. (1992). Communicative virtues and educational relations. In H.A. Alexander (Ed.), *Philosophy of education: Proceedings of the 48th Annual Meeting of the Philosophy of Education Society*, (pp. 34–44). Urbana, Illinois: Philosophy of Education Society.
Ricoeur, P. (1974). Existence and hermeneutics (K. McLaughlin, Trans.). (D. Ihde, Ed.). *The conflict of interpretations: Essays in hermeneutics*. Evanston, IL: Northwestern University Press. (Original work published 1969)

Rivkin, Mary. (1991). Mary's voice. In L.M. Berman et al., *Toward curriculum for being: Voices of educators* (pp. 65–85). Albany: State University of New York Press.

Roche, M. (1973). *Phenomenology, language and the social sciences.* London: Routledge & Kegan Paul.

Rorty, R. (1982). *Consequences of pragmatism.* Minneapolis: University of Minnesota Press.

Ruddick, S. (1989). *Maternal thinking: Toward a politics of peace.* New York: Ballantine Books.

Schempp, P.G., Sparkes A.C., & Templin T.J. (1993). The micropolitics of teacher induction. *American Educational Research Journal 30*(3), 447–472.

Schutz, A. (1967). *The phenomenology of the social world.* (G. Walsh & F. Lehnert, Trans.). Evanston, IL: Northwestern University Press.

Shor, I. (1992). *Empowering education: Critical teaching for social change.* Chicago: University of Chicago Press.

Shor, I., & Freire P. (1987). *A pedagogy for liberation: Dialogues on transforming education.* Westport, CT: Greenwood, Bergin-Garvey.

Silvers, R.J. (1982). A silence within phenomenology. In V. Darroch & R.J. Silvers (Eds.), *Interpretive human studies* (pp. 231–248). Lanham, MD: University Press of America.

Sirotnik, K.A. (1988). What goes on in classrooms? Is this the way we want it? In Beyer, L.E. & Apple, M.W. (Eds.), *The curriculum: Problems, politics, and possibilities.* New York: State University of New York Press.

Slattery, P. (1995). *Curriculum development in the postmodern era.* New York: Garland.

Smith, J.E. (1987). The reconception of experience in Peirce, James, and Dewey. In R.S. Corrington, C. Hausman, & T.M. Seebohn (Eds.). *Pragmatism considers phenomenology* (pp. 73–91). Washington, D.C.: Center for Advanced Research in Phenomenology & University Press of America. .

Stern, L. (1990). Conceptions of separation and connection in female adolescents. In C. Gilligan, N.P. Lyons, & T.J. Hanmer (Eds.). *Making connections: The relational worlds of adolescent girls at Emma Willard School* (pp. 73–87). Cambridge: Harvard University Press.

Stroker, E. (1987). Descriptive phenomenology: Remarks on Husser1's approach to the foundation of knowledge. In L. Hardy (Ed.), *The Husserlian foundations of science* (pp. 15–31). Washington, D.C.: Center for Advanced Research in Phenomenology & University Press of America.

Trueit, D. (2002). Speaking of ghosts. In W.E. Doll & N. Gough (Eds.), *Curriculum visions* (pp. 269–280). New York: Peter Lang.

Vandenberg, D. (1992). Researching lived experiences: A review essay. *Educational Theory, 2*(1), 119–126.

Van Maanen, J. (1988). *Tales of the field: On writing ethnography.* Chicago: University of Chicago Press.

Van Manen, M. (1982). Edifying theory: Serving the good. *Theory into Practice, 21*(1), 44–49.

———. (1984). Practicing phenomenological writing. *Phenomenology and Pedagogy, 21*(1), 36–69.

———. (1990). *Researching lived experience.* Albany: State University of New York Press.

———. (1991). *The tact of teaching: The meaning of pedaqoqica1 thouqhtfulness.* Albany: State University of New York Press.

Walker, A. (1985). *The color purple.* New York: Pocket Books.

Walkerdine, V. (1990). *Schoolgirl fictions.* London: Verso.

Wharton, E. (1984). *The house of mirth.* New York: Bantam Books.

Wolfe, T. (1970). *Look homeward, angel.* New York: Bantam Books. (Original work published 1929).

Wood, G.H. (1990). Teachers as curriculum workers. In J.T. Sears, & J.D. Marshall (Eds.), *Teaching and thinking about curriculum: Critical inquiries* (pp. 97–109). New York: Teachers College Press.

Young, R. (1990). *A critical theory of education: Habermas and our children's future*. New York: Teachers College Press.

Woolf, V. (1978). *The Pargiters: The novel-essay portion of 'the years'*. In M.A. Leaska (Ed.). New York: Harcourt Brace Jovanovich.

INDEX

Complicated Conversation

A BOOK SERIES OF CURRICULUM STUDIES

This series employs research completed in various disciplines to construct textbooks that will enable public school teachers to reoccupy a vacated public domain—not simply as "consumers" of knowledge, but as active participants in a "complicated conversation" that they themselves will lead. In drawing promiscuously but critically from various academic disciplines and from popular culture, this series will attempt to create a conceptual montage for the teacher who understands that positionality as aspiring to reconstruct a "public" space. *Complicated Conversation* works to resuscitate the progressive project—an educational project in which self-realization and democratization are inevitably intertwined; its task as the new century begins is nothing less than the intellectual formation of a public sphere in education.

The series editor is:

Dr. William F. Pinar
Department of Curriculum and Instruction
223 Peabody Hall
Louisiana State University
Baton Rouge, LA 70803-4728